ITALY
from the Air

ITALY
from the Air

Folco Quilici

Weidenfeld and Nicolson · London

Acknowledgments

The author would like to thank Luca Tamagnini for his technical expertise and his company.

The publishers are grateful to Susan and David Worth of Line & Line for the maps which appear on pages 6, 14, 58 and 103.

First published in Great Britain in 1987 by
George Weidenfeld and Nicolson Ltd
91 Clapham High Street
London SW4 7TA

ISBN 0 297 79014 5

Designed by Helen Lewis

Filmset by Deltatype, Ellesmere Port, South Wirral
Colour separations by Newsele Litho SPA, Italy
Printed and bound by LEGO, Vicenza, Italy

half-title The desolate island of Lampedusa, largest of the Pelagic group, its rock face scorched bare by the heat of the sun, lies midway between Malta and Tunisia, nearer Africa than Europe.

title page The fortress village of Giglio Castello, built on the highest point of the small Tuscan island of Giglio in the Tyrrhenian Sea.

Contents

Introduction

I have been flying over Italy's coasts and cities, mountains and valleys for almost twenty years. I still find it a joy and a thrill to fly over the landscape of my native country, and I have often wondered why the pleasure never wanes, why it is so gratifying and yet never completely satisfying.

There is clearly something very individual in looking at the world from a helicopter: it is a bird's-eye view but quite different from the prospect you get from an aeroplane. Flying in a helicopter is like having a marvellous ride on horseback, albeit on a winged, gravity-defying horse. It is not an air voyage in the usual sense. The flights we are accustomed to in aeroplanes take us through the sky at great heights and speed. The landscape rapidly unreels beneath the wings like a map rendered in hazy, indefinable colours. A helicopter is never very far from the ground – our plexiglass cabin often skims right over houses and tree tops – and the speed is fairly modest (never more than fifty miles per hour in the kind of helicopter generally used for aerial photography).

The combination of low altitude and low speed means that the landscape unrolls in images that are not distant and abstract, like those seen from an aeroplane, but close up – you can almost touch them. That is why it seems appropriate to compare a helicopter with a horse. Travelling by helicopter is what horseback travel used to be: you can move freely, not bound to the itinerary established by a road or railway, or an air lane thirty thousand feet up in the sky. In the past a horseback rider looked at the world from a modest height, granted, but nevertheless from above, and was not obliged to follow the course of a public thoroughfare, as carriages and coaches were. When he felt like it, the rider could jump a hedge, cross a thick wood or ford a river without path or bridge. And that is exactly what a helicopter does, only much more quickly and easily.

For some years now Luca Tamagnini has been flying with me, adding his own views to our archives. He is at one of the open doors and I am at the other, and between us is an assistant, barely able to move between lens cases, packs of film, and bags of spare camera parts. The pilot is fully occupied in following our route, dealing with the wind, and avoiding off-limit zones.

Not infrequently we have touched down in country farmyards, grazed the balconies of city dwellings, and come close enough to people to gauge their facial expressions. In the countryside dogs often chase our shadow, leaping over hedges and barking their heads off; and chickens flurry up in a cloud of white and black feathers as if in fear of being trampled under a horse's hooves when the wind of the rotor alarms them.

One day we were flying over Tropea, a Calabrian town sited on top of a sheer rock cliff on the edge of the Tyrrhenian Sea. People came out on their balconies and leaned out of windows to watch us go by as we dipped below houses perched high over the sea. As a sign of greeting, I imagine, they threw sheets of paper, empty cardboard boxes, and even a kitchen plate at us. Fortunately the plate did not hit the cabin or it would have shattered

the glass. On another occasion I nearly crashed after being caught unawares by a child's kite.

Dangerous or not, this is still a remarkable job. Poking your head out of the door of a small Bell helicopter, looking at the world spread out before you through the sights of a movie or still camera, you experience incomparable sensations, especially when you are involved in a kind of storytelling in pictures: the feeling, for example of being so close to the peak of Mount Cervino that it is almost within reach, and then veering round to see the whole range of the western Alps. You can come so close to the walls of a castle that you can see where the plaster has cracked and green moss sprouts between the cusps of the merlons, and at the same time encompass the view of all the surrounding territory. There is a similar sensation over the Strait of Messina: the prow of a swordfish boat cuts through the water right beneath you, and simultaneously the horizon extends in an infinite curve like a shining mirror.

But beyond the personal joy and the professional satisfaction there is something else, something much more important, that makes flying over Italy inexhaustibly interesting: this land is a mosaic or, rather, it consists of layer upon layer of civilization and cultural cross-breeding. The hundreds and thousands of disparate elements from the past that make up contempory life can be clearly interpreted from a helicopter. It provides a vantage point from which the world below can be scanned as easily as reading a map.

An archaeological site, a Renaissance palace or a road laid out by Roman legionaries and urbanized in the Middle Ages are all redolent of their period, and so much of the past remains that when we plan an itinerary for a helicopter flight we can choose one that carries us back to the age of Caesar or Lucrezia Borgia, to Galileo's time or Garibaldi's.

Considering its size, the little town of Maróstica, north-east of Vicenza, is protected by impressive defensive works. Castellated walls and towers encircle it, climbing the hill to a castle stategically placed on the highest point. Built by the Scaliger family of Verona, the castle and its ramparts date from the fourteenth century.

While the coastal cities feared invasion from the south, the whole of the north of Italy, and especially the eastern part, was studded with cities armed for defence against the devastating raids of Germanic hordes from the north and Magyar and Slav attack from the east.

The helicopter might even pass for a time machine out of a story by H.G. Wells: it can take you through the pages of history, lifting you out of the real world and setting you down (sometimes by chance but more often by choice) in another age.

Other ages do still exist, at least in part, if you know how to look for them. If you choose the right itinerary, the helicopter can transport you to shores that are thousands of years away yet still spread out between familiar lands and seas. There is a kind of magic in this: a helicopter flight can be a voyage through history more than through geography. You can fly into the past and find that it co-exists with the present, hidden but waiting to be evoked. It can be a stunning experience when a time that seemed gone

forever suddenly re-emerges so vividly that it erases all the boundless and often tiresome signs of the present. The past comes so alive that remote events seem to have just occurred.

I remember a flight over the Arbia River and Montaperti in Tuscany. I had gone to photograph the little stream and the cypress-covered hill nearby, where the Sienese and the Florentines waged a fierce battle on 4 September 1260, the battle that Dante tells us 'dyed the Arbia red'. When I had finished photographing from the air I asked the pilot to land on the battle site. I wanted to supplement the aerial stills and film with a photograph of the commemorative pillar on the ground. We landed in a field where the grain had only recently been harvested. An old man in shirtsleeves and a grey waistcoat stopped his work in a neighbouring field to come over and see what I was doing. He saw that I was photographing the battle monument, and after a long silence he burst forth in an unmistakably Sienese accent, 'They could have done much better; they should have pressed on right away . . . right away.' When he got no reaction to his remarks he went on: 'Let me tell you, seeing as how everything went well, and considering the lesson we gave *them*, we should have chased them all the way home and smashed everything they had. Don't you think so?' He nodded at the hill I was photographing, as if to dispel any possible doubt that he was talking about the thirteenth-century victory of the Sienese at Montaperti. And the 'them' was clearly the Florentines. He talked about it as if the battle had been fought not seven centuries earlier but only a few weeks or even hours before.

The pictures I took that day at Montaperti I showed subsequently in Siena. When the slides of the hill and the river appeared on the screen there was a buzz of whispering in the hall and a sudden surge of emotion – the sort of response that only a very recent event can arouse. Evidently Siena, like other historic Italian cities that are caught up in their traditions, regards local history as if it were all but contemporary. It is not just historic sites and monuments that summon up this sort of feeling, nor is it only theatrical and traditional public commemorations, like Siena's *Palio*, that evoke such a strong reaction. Unexpected images can have the same effect: aerial photographs have a special ability to recall the past and 'erase time', and they can bring strong collective memories back to life, memories that have smouldered for generations but never been totally extinguished.

To mention a vivid personal recollection, I once flew over the *crete*, those grooved clay mounds that mark the rolling countryside of central Italy. From the helicopter it took just one glance to embrace not only those lunar slopes but also the other hills in those valleys, hills that seem to have been created solely as backgrounds to miniature paintings: two typical but antithetical aspects of that countryside. From the ground, looking up, they are distinct and contrasting features; from the sky, looking down, they balance and blend into one another, forming a single landscape that no painter has ever captured.

I have another recollection from that same working day. We were flying in lazy curves over the bare white backs of those *crete* when a man appeared on horseback. It was as if horse and rider were set against the background of the famous portrait of Guidoriccio da Fogliano by Simone Martini in Siena's Palazzo Pubblico. Their path took man and horse through the shade of the rolling hills; the burnt colour of summer around them was offset by the dark green of the nearby hedges and the distant olive trees. Horse and rider

From the air the most striking characteristic of the central Italian landscape is the alternation of wide stretches of bare chalk hills – known as *crete* – with some of the most intensely cultivated farmland in the entire peninsula. This is typical of the country near Siena.

disappeared as suddenly as they had appeared, into a thick stand of oak trees. The landscape was once again deserted, but the thrill of the encounter remained.

From the sky Italy often provides images that cannot be appreciated from the ground, particularly now that the living museum that Italy used to be has been transformed and partly devastated by progress. Scenes of nature from famous medieval Italian paintings seem to appear more sharply and more frequently when you are flying over deserted countryside, and over villages where the simple shapes of cottages and slender lines of towers and belfries can barely be distinguished through morning mist. There is a harmony of regular spaces and rhythms from above: one sees the landscape not as city versus countryside, the way things are now, but as city *and* countryside, as they were at the time of the great Italian communes and *signorie*. That time is very remote from the age in which I live, and I have the helicopter to thank for making it possible to observe this rare and precious survival.

I owe the helicopter gratitude for another opportunity as well, an important one for someone interested in knowing and documenting Italy – not only the Italy of nature but also the Italy created through the efforts of man. The architect or city planner responsible for a cathedral, a castle or an urban area makes a flat plan that provides in one glance an overall view, just as one has from the air. I have had a chance to appreciate the architect's original conception from that vantage point, seeing his work laid out below me exactly as he planned it on the drawing board. When the helicopter is used as an instrument of documentation it becomes a means of creating a unique and unmistakable language of images. The plan of an old and complex agricultural area, for example, or a city plan seen from the air are very different from imagining them on the ground. When you read the plan of a city or a landscape from the air you can call up the spirit of past civilizations, the culture, history, reality, and even the folly of the people who built that area, lived in it and transformed it.

To discover the world from the sky is almost intoxicating at times. No matter how often you have flown with a camera in your hand, the day never comes when you can say 'One day is just like another; I've seen it all. I'm no longer interested in taking pictures from the sky.' It never becomes mere routine, there is always something to discover, some new sensation to experience. I still feel the excitement that I felt on my first photographic flight. Years of experience have gradually given me greater technical self-assurance, but this has been offset by increasing uncertainty: how do you translate an idea into an image, transform a concept into a picture? I do not consider this uncertainty something negative; it is the doubt born of the possibility of choice. I have had constantly to expand my vocabulary of images, to find new points of view in an attempt to interpret the multiplicity of attitudes, cultures, lifestyles and landscapes that make up this country of mine. I owe this rather ample confession to anyone interested in looking at my photographs. There are no technical secrets behind them. There is simply an enormous, sometimes contradictory, and often polemical passion for Italy.

Folco Quilici
Rome, 1986

Palermo. A sight to been seen all over Italy today – magnificent villas of the eighteenth century decaying under the onslaught of unbridled building speculation. In Sicily densely populated new areas are often financed by recycled 'dirty money' from the new Mafia, an issue afflicting many of the southern provinces of Italy.

TRENTINO-
ALTO ADIGE

Lake Resia
● Glorenza

*Altopiano
del Renon*   *Alpe di Siusi*
Bolzano ●   ▲   ▲ *Gruppo di Sella*

DOLOMITES   FRIULI-
                      VENEZIA
                      GIULIA
● Trento

River Adige   *River Piave*

Lake Como

Lake Maggiore   BERGAMO ALPS   Udine ●

Mont Blanc ▲ *Mount Cervino*   *Borromean Islands*   VENETIAN ALPS   Palmanova ●
▲ Courmayeur   *Lake Orta*   Maróstica
  ● Aosta   Bergamo ●   *Lake Iseo*   Cittadella ●   Trieste ●
VALLE   Merate ●   Vicenza ● ● Treviso
D'AOSTA   ● Bard   Padua ● ● Torcello
                                       Milan ●   Brescia ●   *Lake Garda*   Verona ●   ● Venice
GRAIAN ALPS   Novara ●   LOMBARDY   *Gulf of Venice*
              River Ticino   VENETO
        Vercelli ●   Solferino ●
                                                River Adda
Venaria Reale ●   *River Po*   ● Pavia   Mantua ●
Turin ●   Cremona ●   *River Adige*
       PIEDMONT   Piacenza ●   *River Po*
                 River Tanaro ● Alessandria   *Po di Maestra*
COTTIAN ALPS   Parma ●   ● Ferrara

                                              EMILIA ROMAGNA   ● Modena
              LIGURIA ● Genoa   *Valli di Comacchio*
                            Gulf of Genoa   Bologna ●
                                                                        ● Ravenna
                                                    A P E N N I N E S
Apricale ● ● Cervo   ● La Spezia
      Bussana Vecchia   *L I G U R I A N   S E A*

The North

I sat in a large hall at the National Air and Space Museum in Washington and saw the whole of northern Italy from the sky. On a giant screen they were showing films taken from the dizzying altitude of the space shuttle. One glance took in all of the Po valley gripped in the semicircle of the Alps and the Apennines. The valley was like an enormous footprint, a deep impression with high splayed edges, stamped on the south of Europe. The narrator's voice remarked that this was the 'country where Columbus was born' (Genoa was a speck on the shimmering edge of the Tyrrhenian Sea), 'the land where Marco Polo was born . . .' (I tried to imagine the area east of the great plain and the water in the Venetian lagoon).

I grew up on the banks of the Po. It was like the Nile or the Mississippi or the Amazon to me. But the view from the space shuttle made my mighty river look like a poor little garter snake twisting along a small valley. There are twenty million people who live on the Po plain now that it is totally urbanized. I used to be one of their number, and I too started and ended almost every day with a haze of mist in the summer and a fog in the winter. This is an unmistakable feature of my beloved north. I had a global view of the fog one morning on a flight back from the United States. The jumbo jet was some thirty thousand feet above the western Alps. One minute I could see the whole Po valley out of the window to my left; the next it seemed to vanish under my feet, disappearing altogether towards the east. Inside the semicircle of Alpine and Apennine peaks it looked like a boiling kettle. Fog covered the entire plain; it might have been an enormous lake whose waters had been transformed into a kind of ethereal foam. I have ended up in that foam often enough. I have almost been lost in it on helicopter flights over Piedmont, Lombardy, Emilia and especially the Veneto region.

Out of a host of striking recollections I remember one particularly magic moment when an apparition broke through that steamy curtain. We were heading south-east from Udine, flying over vineyards that were already rust-streaked with autumn. All of a sudden the fog thickened and enveloped us menacingly, but through a small clear patch we glimpsed below us the Villa Manin at Passariano, the country home of the last doge of Venice. At that very moment the radio voice that was the constant companion on all our flights, croaked at us: 'No landing at the airport. The field is fogged in . . . visibility zero.' The pilot thought for a moment and decided to land near the villa. He would wait on the ground until the radio gave us authorization to go back to the airfield.

A soft dip, and the rotor cut less violently through the damp air. We started down into the middle of the large amphitheatre-like space that opens out in front of the villa. When we were only inches above the ground I photographed the sleek green grass beneath us. But we did not touch down. At the last moment the pilot changed his mind. He gunned the engine cheerfully and we rose up in the air again. 'I have a better idea', he announced over the intercom. Two minutes later he had set us down in a clearing between two vineyards to the rear of the great house.

We had a view of the villa between the yellowing leaves of the grapevines, which glowed in the leaden light and contrasted with the washed-out white of the façade of the building. Two local people came up to us and a boy appeared, bouncing over the grass on a motorbike. 'If we had landed a month ago there would have been grapes to eat', the pilot remarked. 'The grapes are finished, but we've got must', another voice answered. It was suddenly clear why the pilot had changed his landing site. 'New wine is good for you . . . especially when the fog is coming on, and it's turning cold.' Before one could ask for it, a sparkling new wine had been produced. A good bottle of wine may not be a substitute for a good radar system if you want a safe flight, but it certainly combats the icy chill of the Bell's cabin when you are flying with the door wide open.

On another autumn day of sudden swirling fog we flew over one of the many walled cities of northern Italy, the opulent town of Cittadella in the Veneto region. The flowing wall surrounding it looked amazingly irrregular. It is a narrow but solid structure standing some forty feet tall and running between houses and fields; after more than seven and a half centuries there is not a single breach in the whole wall. It is just as it was when its peasant architect Benvenuto di Cartura erected it in the thirteenth century. I thought it would have been nice to have him with me in the helicopter that day. I would have liked to show him something he was never able to see himself, the overall design of his completed wall from the air. I thought he would have enjoyed the ride and might well have given himself a pat on the back. The fog caught us over Cittadella. It was a thick white veil that seemed to rise out of the ploughed fields below. The landscape seemed to shift from reality into a dream world. In a few minutes all that was visible was the very top of Benvenuto di Cartura's walls. It was like scalloped lace in a white sea of vapour, but a vapour that was not transparent; it was as dense as the clouds in Mantegna's painting of Saint Sebastian. It floated in the sky as if made of some mysterious substance that was solid and impalpable at the same time. Luckily, these fantasies were mine alone and had no effect whatsoever on the pilot, who had a great deal of experience of flying in this area where dense fog can descend in no time at all. He knew his business and was a model of professionalism.

The fog in the Po valley hides everyone and everything for two hundred days in the year. It descends and thickens and curtains the world so thickly that you can see only a few feet ahead of you and can ignore the rest of the world. There is an advantage in all of this, and as a native-born son of northern Italy I have tried to make the most of this negative feature of my homeland – not by taking photographs but by using my eyes, by looking around and taking in my immediate surroundings. I have tried to look at northern Italy region by region and piece by piece, and to see it the way it was before it was standardized and made uniform in modern times by political administration and town planning.

Northern Italy is not a composite territory united around a single capital; it is a homogeneous area divided among a hundred capitals. And a great many of those capitals have preserved signs of former splendour in the surviving elements of their urban plan or in specific buildings and monuments. These relics can be seen in a particularly striking and fascinating way from the sky, especially when wings of fog cancel out some of the banalities that characterize and standardize the modern world. Looking down from the sky you can concentrate on the details that give quality and distinction to a city, those features that enable one to say, look, that is the Mantua of the Gonzagas, that is Savoyard Turin, the Venice of the doges, the Dorias' Genoa, Milan at the time of the Viscontis, the Ferrara made famous by the Dukes of Este, Bourbon and Napoleonic Parma, Ravenna under the Byzantine governors. This flowering of hundreds of dominant cities, it is worth repeating, was the glory and the ruin not only of northern Italy but of the whole peninsula, its grandeur and its misfortune.

Nowadays we are beginning to realize that this lack of unity and uniformity and this plurality of centres of power and influence were the source of an extremely positive development, Italy's current experiment in regional independence; it now seems like a healthy antidote to the all-devouring centralism of a single absolute capital (consider the role of Paris in relation to provincial France).

If my only view of the Po valley had been the one from outer space, I would have been left with a single impression of that vast and complex area, a uniform image flattened out by distance, a geographical image untouched by man. But turning to detail, and ignoring the monotonous mass of building blocks that might equally well be located in Frankfurt or Detroit, Manchester or Lyons, I think my northern Italy has a look all its own. Its cultural pluralism would entitle it to a motto on its escutcheon if it had a coat of arms (the north is proletarian rather than noble). The motto is old, abused, and perhaps unfashionable, but true nevertheless: unity in diversity.

The Western Alps, Valle d'Aosta

The rock barrier of the Alps above
Courmayeur, north-west of Aosta: this
dramatically beautiful region of thick pine
forests, meadows, rivers and waterfalls is
enclosed by high peaks along its borders
with France and Switzerland. When Italy
was under threat from the north they
provided an impressive natural defence
system, deep valleys being the sole means of
access. The area has always been inhabited
by people of a fiercely independent spirit; in
the past they fought relentlessly against
attempts by forces from both north and
south to dominate their passes.

Under the Italian Constitution of 1945
the Valle d'Aosta has an independent
charter within the republic: the region is
bilingual, French and Italian.

Castles of the Valle d'Aosta

Between the Rànzola and Challant gorges
north of Bard, on the winding Alpine route
between northern and southern Europe, are
the ruins of the thirteenth-century castle of
Graines. Perched high on a crag over the
small town of Arcesaz, it clearly shows how
this landscape offered perfect sites for the
construction of invincible fortresses.

The mighty castle of Fénis, east of Aosta, is
one of the finest in the region. It was largely
rebuilt in about 1340 for Aymon de
Challant, and has recently been restored to
its original splendour. It was well designed
for the period, massive and solidly built
(Ghibelline castellations crown inner and
outer walls), but its powerful defences are
balanced by features more fitted to elegant
living – a central courtyard and windows
over the valley.

Bard castle dominates the southern end of the Aosta valley, in the narrow Gorge de Bard. Built in the eleventh century on Roman foundations, it was transformed in the thirteenth century by Amedeo IV of Savoy, and reconstructed after Napoleon had almost entirely destroyed it in the first half of the nineteenth century.

This cannon-proof military garrison, a new development in castle design, is quite different in style from the turreted structures built for siege tactics.

Aosta, Valle d'Aosta

The city of Aosta, the capital of the region, was already a flourishing centre two thousand years ago: an entire Roman legion was stationed here, and Rome was the first major power to dominate the valley and establish its hegemony over the St Bernard Pass, the main route north towards Gaul. The Roman theatre once seated over three thousand spectators (its great rear wall still stands seventy-two feet high), and there are other relics of Roman dominion here – the ruined east gate, the Arch of Augustus (a memorial to the city's founder) and much of the original city wall.

21

Turin and Venaria Reale, Piedmont

The Piedmont region, once part of the kingdom of Savoy, has a dual aspect: one is the prosperous, industrialized, outward-looking face of the area around Turin – one of the most progressive cities in Italy; the other is the old provincial face of small communities whose life and culture depend relatively little on outside influences.

Turin (*left*), the capital of Piedmont, and of all Italy for a brief period (1861–5), lies on the left bank of the Po, with a backcloth of the Cottian and Graian Alps. It is a French-style city, largely nineteenth century, dominated by the 548-foot-high Mole Antonelliana, begun in 1863 as a synagogue and extended upwards as a tower in 1878. It now houses the Risorgimento Museum. Like Milan, the suburbs of Turin are ever-expanding as southerners pour in in search of work. South of the city, in Lingotto, is the main Fiat works (founded in 1899), which employs over 150,000 people and has a test circuit on the roof of the factory.

By contrast there are small towns such as Venaria Reale (*below left*), places seemingly untouched by events or even fashions. The elegant crescent-shaped mansion was built as a royal hunting-lodge *c.* 1660 and restored by B. Alfieri and the great Sicilian architect Filippo Juvarra in 1714–28.

The Stupinigi Palace, Piedmont

The Palazzina di Caccia at Stupinigi *(right)* was built for Victor Amadeus II in 1729–30. From the air Filippo Juvarra's elegant and ingenious design for this baroque extravaganza can be seen to full advantage: the mansion was built for the pleasures of the hunt and its plan imitates the head and horns of a deer. But it has always been far more a palace than a hunting lodge, providing a spectacular setting for grand receptions, weddings and balls. Napoleon stayed here on several occasions. Set in acres of magnificent gardens and parkland on the outskirts of Turin, the building now houses a museum of art and furniture.

Piedmontese rice fields

The Vercelli area of Piedmont, roughly
midway between Milan and Turin, is the
largest rice-growing region in Europe. A
wide, watery landscape, it lies in the heart
of the Po valley, irrigated by melted snow
from the Alps. It is the land of the *mondine*,
women who harvested the rice by hand
before mechanical means were introduced,
working eight hours a day, three months of
the year, standing thigh-deep in water.

Lake Orta and its island, Piedmont

All the northern Italian lakes were born at
the end of the Ice Age and are fed by the
surviving Alpine glaciers. These lakes form a
delicately balanced ecosystem which gives
the Po valley its humid climate and fertility.

   The island of San Giulio in Lake Orta
was once shunned as the haunt of serpents;
now it contains villas and gardens of the
Milanese aristocracy. At the centre of the
tightly clustered buildings is an enormous
seminary, and next to it a church
traditionally said to have been founded in
390 by St Julius, who purged the island of
its snakes.

This vast and elegant mansion in Merate, west of Bergamo, is one of the best known villas of Lombardy. Grand country houses such as this were designed with two ends in mind: they were meant to provide a setting for the pleasures of life in society and for the joys of solitude, to be experienced not separately but together.

The Villa Belgioioso was built for the Signor Marchese Novati, Gentleman of the Bedchamber to the Queen of Hungary and Bohemia, in the early eighteenth century.

Isola Bella, Piedmont

Floating serenely on the clear, cold waters of Lake Maggiore is the Isola Bella, one of the four Borromean Islands – named after the aristocratic Borromeo family to whom three of them belong.

Their beautiful surroundings have made all of them famous, but the Isola Bella, originally a barren rock with a small village on it, is the most spectacular. Count Charles III Borromeo decided in 1630 to transform

it in honour of his wife, Isabella. He swept away the village and set about creating a suitably opulent island paradise, bringing boatloads of earth from the mainland to make a garden of ten terraces descending regally to the water's edge; statuary and ornamental urns, towers, pavilions and fountains, rare plants and white peacocks were then added to this sumptuous display. A baroque palace with a collection of fine furniture, which is open to the public, completes the whole remarkable edifice.

Milan, Lombardy

The church of Sant'Ambrogio, Milan's Romanesque masterpiece, with twin bell-towers and cloisters, dominates the foreground of this view of Milan. It was originally built as a martyrs' basilica between 379 and 386. At the front is an atrium in the form of an arcaded courtyard, a rare and remarkable feature which dates, in its present form, from 1150.

The essayist Guido Piovene called the city 'a utilitarian metropolis that has been demolished and rebuilt over the centuries, depending on the needs of the moment, but it has never managed to be authentically old'. The 'utilitarian metropolis' can clearly be seen in the background. Milan is Italy's major industrial city – a producer of textiles, machinery, chemicals and paper. It lies near the southern end of passes through the Alps, in the fertile Lombardy plain, and its position had made it significant even before the Romans came.

The Certosa di Pavia, Lombardy

Founded by Gian Galeazzo Visconti in 1396 as a family mausoleum, this great Carthusian monastery, ranged round a series of courtyards and cloisters, is a treasure-house of the Lombardy quattrocento.

Behind can be seen the magnificent monastery church, completed in 1472; its carved and sculpted marble façade, a later addition, is considered a masterpiece of northern Italian architecture of the early Renaissance. In the foreground stretches the wide green expanse of the Great Cloister, with the monks' quarters on three sides, each cell consisting of two small rooms and a little garden below, a loggia and a bedroom above.

The consistency of style, the liveliness of the architecture, and the mellow rich red of the roof tiles give this beautiful monastic complex a special sense of unity, enhanced by the way the buildings blend into the serene and infinite Lombardy plain.

Solferino, Lombardy

A commemorative chapel stands on the site
of the 1859 battle between the Italians and
the Austrians, the bloodiest encounter of
Italy's struggle for independence. This
memorial was unveiled in 1959 in honour
of the Swiss philanthropist Jean Henri
Dunant. Horrified by the sufferings of the
wounded at the battle of Solferino, he laid
on relief medical services – and his
dedicated humanitarian work was to be the
beginnings of the international Red Cross.
He fostered the first Geneva convention for
prisoners of war and was the first winner of
the Nobel peace prize.

Riviera di Levante, Liguria

Towering over the sea above the Gulf of
Tigullio is the sanctuary of Our Lady of
Monte Allegro. Ligurian sailors used to
scale the heights barefoot from the port in
thanks for returning safely from
Mediterranean and Atlantic crossings.

Cervo, Liguria

The flamboyant baroque church in the little town of Cervo, on the Riviera di Ponente: according to the novelist Italo Calvino, who was born in this region of Italy, 'its façade is like a sail stretched by the wind of the Ligurian Sea'. The graceful curves of its west front face out to sea, and were designed to be seen by sailors in passing ships.

The picturesque little town shelters in a valley of the Apennines, whose green hills stretch down to the shoreline just below the church.

Genoa, Liguria

At the height of its maritime glory Genoa competed with Venice as Italy's most illustrious port and commercial centre. Its ships and merchants traded all over Europe, and it is still on a par with Marseilles as a major Mediterranean seaport. Few relics of that victorious past can be found today as the new city expands at the expense of the old, but even now there are more splendid palaces here than in any other Italian city; it was from their opulence and grandeur that Genoa derived the name 'La Superba'. Its position, in a natural amphitheatre at the head of the Ligurian Sea, not only gave it its maritime power, but also helped to make it a strikingly beautiful city.

The Piazzo De Ferrari, at the centre, mostly built in the nineteenth century, is surrounded on all sides by impressive baroque-style buildings – public monuments, the offices of big shipping lines and banks – with all the busiest streets converging on it. On the right is the curved, arcaded façade of the neo-baroque Stock Exchange, the Borsa, and beyond it the Accademia Linguistica di Belle Arte, which houses a library and a fine collection of paintings by Ligurian artists.

Seen from the air, Bussana Vecchia seems a total ruin; it was in fact deserted after a catastrophic earthquake in 1887. In recent years, however, the crumbling and for the most part ownerless houses have become the refuge of a group of foreign and Italian painters and craftsmen who run their own independent community.

Apricale, Liguria

Apricale clings to an olive-covered spur on the lower slopes of the Alpi Marittime. The warm grey stone houses seem to have been piled on top of each other, with huge pillars and porticoes to support them, as they climb up the hillside linked by arched passageways, steps and narrow streets.

Until a few years ago, a medieval bridge across the valley was the only means of access to the town, which was once the centre of a flourishing farming district. Now the place is virtually abandoned. It may be for this very reason that it is the most striking medieval town in the Ligurian hills.

The Dolomites, Trentino-Alto Adige

The jagged rock walls and toothed crags of
the Sella group and the Gardena valley, like
the rest of this Alpine area, were created
two hundred million years ago. At that time
the primordial Mediterranean Sea known as
the 'Tethys' extended from Africa to eastern
Europe, forming atolls of madrepore and
other corals over about a hundred million
years. In a series of inconceivably violent
volcanic shocks the sea floor was raised to a
higher level, and the Alps and Dolomites
emerged from the waves. The mountains
owe their colour to veins of coral from the
old sea bed, and their name to the
concentrations of dolomitic rock, impacted,
buckled and twisted by the movement of the
earth's plates.

Trentino-Alto Adige

Though the Alto Adige is geographically Italian, its ethnic majority is German (the German-speakers call the region 'South Tyrol'), and a substantial Alpine population still speak the Tyrolean dialect of Ladin.

Opposite above A typical Alto Adige landscape – the valleys and mountains of the Dolomites, where Ladin is still spoken. The photograph was taken over the Seiser Alm, or Alpe di Siusi.

Opposite below Bolzano, Italy's most northerly city, and the capital of this small area since 1927; its population is largely German-speaking, and the cathedral with its twin towers is unmistakably German in style.

Below Much of northern Italy's hydroelectric power is produced by artificial lakes in the Alps. Lake Resia, a recently created reservoir, has not yet blended fully into the Alpine landscape: it will probably give rise to feelings of disquiet as long as the belfry of a church, submerged when the water swallowed up an entire town, can be seen above the surface.

Altopiano del Renon, Trentino-Alto Adige

Pinnacles and peaks created by thousands of years of erosion have given the Renon valley the look of a landscape from another world. These are the so-called 'pyramids' of the Adige Alps: freezes, thaws, water and winds have sculpted the rock into tall, slender spires, leaving huge boulders delicately poised on their topmost points.

Glorenza, Trentino-Alto Adige

The typically Tyrolean town of Glorenza in the Pusteria valley is enclosed in a perfect circuit of walls, erected in the sixteenth century to protect it from attack from the north.

At the four corners, and at intervals along the walls, are guard towers and fortified gatehouses, all in an immaculate state of preservation.

Palmanova, Friuli-Venezia Giulia

The fortified city of Palmanova is laid out
on a plan that can be fully appreciated only
from the sky. The architect Savorgnan
created a nine-point star design, a regular
polygon with eighteen sides and projecting
corners, with six major streets radiating
from a six-sided piazza at its centre.

Founded by the Venetians as a bulwark
against Turkish attack, the city's first stone
was solemnly set down on 7 October 1593,
the twenty-second anniversary of the Battle
of Lepanto. A superb example of military
engineering, Palmanova was long regarded
as the strongest fortress town in Europe; it
was not defeated until the French took it in
1797. In 1960 the entire city was declared a
national monument.

The Veneto Alps

The Veneto region extends from the
Austrian border to the Po valley, its
northern reaches rising to the dramatic
snow-covered peaks of the Dolomites and
Venetian Alps in the province of Belluno.
The whole of southern Veneto consists of a
fertile plain irrigated by rivers flowing off
the Alpine glaciers. The Piave rises here,
carrying melt water down the lower slopes
to the plains, and on to its mouth in the
Gulf of Venice.

Verona, Veneto

The Castelvecchio and the Ponte Scaligero, which spans the Adige river, were built for Cangrande II Delle Scala, overlord of Verona, in the mid-fourteenth century. Family feuds about a hundred years earlier, on which *Romeo and Juliet* is based, had torn the city in two, but in 1260 with the rise to power of the great Ghibelline dynasty of the Scaligers, of which Cangrande was a member, Verona's internal strife was gradually replaced by calm and increasing prosperity.

The Scaligers ruled Verona until 1387, through the most brilliant period of its history, but were finally overthrown and expelled by the tyrant Gian Galeazzo Visconti. In 1405 the city passed into the hands of Venice.

The Ponte Scaligero, with its fine Ghibelline castellations, was almost totally destroyed by bombing during the Second World War and only recently rebuilt.

Maróstica, Veneto

The tradition of the live chess game, a biennial event in Maróstica, dates back to 1545 and began with a love affair: Taddeo Parisio, governor of Maróstica, persuaded the two rivals for the hand of his daughter, Madonna Leonora, to duel with chessmen rather than swords to decide who should win her hand. Her suitors, Vieri da Vallonara (black) and Rinaldo da Angarano (white), played out their duel in the field outside the castle. It is re-enacted today in the main piazza, overlooked by the medieval castle of the Scaliger family on the hill above the town.

The island of Torcello, Veneto

This octagonal church on the island of Torcello, in a lonely part of the Venetian lagoon, was built in the eleventh century in memory of Saint Fosca who was martyred in Ravenna.

The fields and orchards round the building have been cultivated by the monks since they first established their community here. Isolated monastic sites such as this were not only religious and cultural centres; they also played a fundamental role in the transformation of the surrounding territory. The inhospitable malarial marshland of these islands, where Venice grew up, were slowly drained, cultivated and made habitable through the work of generations of medieval monks.

The Villa Rotonda, Veneto

Palladio's masterpiece was built in the latter half of the sixteenth century, as a belvedere for Cardinal Capra, on a delightful hilltop sight outside Vicenza. It is a perfect example of Renaissance architecture, recalling the temples of ancient Greece, with a circular domed core surrounded by four classical porches. Its symmetry and elegant proportions inspired a host of eighteenth-century architects, among them Lord Burlington of Chiswick House in London.

It is the most famous of a number of villas built between the sixteenth and eighteenth centuries along the banks of the Brenta river, an area that until that time had seen only simple straw-roofed peasants' houses, and it reflected an entirely new concept in domestic architecture: it was designed specifically for the enjoyment of its natural surroundings.

Venice, Veneto

Venice stands on an archipelago of 117
islets, separated by a maze of waterways
and linked by elegant bridges. By the
fourteenth century it had become the most
powerful of Italy's republics, dominating the
Adriatic Sea and controlling all the major
trade routes between Europe and the East.

Through its links with the East it had
developed as a centre of Byzantine art, later
absorbing the influences of Lombardy
Romanesque and Gothic to produce a style
of architecture that is characteristically
Venetian.

The palaces along the Grand Canal, seen
here at its elbow turn above the Accademia
Bridge, range from the thirteenth to the
nineteenth centuries, but they have a
homogeneity which contributes greatly to
the charm and grace of this remarkable city.
They were built for rich merchants and the
aristocrats of the Venetian Republic, many
of them patrons of the artists who brought
Venice to its highest point: the Renaissance
produced a school of Venetian painters that
included Giorgione, Veronese, Titian,
Tintoretto and the Bellinis.

A Venetian street market (above)

A glimpse of life on market day in the
Piazza Santa Maria Formosa, in the Castello
district of Venice. The tourists are away,
and the square belongs to the local
population, at least for a few hours.

The Gulf of Venice, Veneto

The fishery at Ca Zane near Chioggia, at the southern end of the Venetian lagoon. The continuous interaction of cold water tides – rich in plankton – from the Adriatic with the warmer waters of the Gulf of Venice has made this a rich fishing area since prehistoric times. But today the dumping of industrial waste is a cause of increasing pollution of the Upper Adriatic and a serious threat to the ecology of the lagoon.

Valli di Comacchio, Emilia Romagna

The so-called *valli* at the mouth of the Po river teem with eels on their way to their breeding grounds thousands of miles away in the Sargasso Sea. Tons of them are caught in the delta, in eel traps suspended in wide sheets of brackish water separated by dykes. In winter the *valli* are invaded by clouds of wild geese and migrant duck who feed off the eels and other fish, such as carp and pike, which inhabit the waters of the Po. At that time of the year the flat marshlands and river banks vanish for days at a time beneath a dense layer of fog which hangs heavily over the icy water.

The *valli* are a geographical and ecological continuation of the Venetian lagoon, and they are suffering many of the same problems. The river gathers up the sewage of the entire Po valley, the waste of some twenty million people across the whole of northern Italy, building up huge quantities of silt at its mouth and making the waters among the most polluted in Europe. A range of products is now being tested in an endeavour to clean up the delta.

Ravenna and the Po delta, Emilia Romagna

Under Emperor Honorius the seat of government of the Western Empire was established in Ravenna in AD 404, and after barbarian raids and sackings (Theodoric the Ostrogoth held it from 493 to 526) the town became the capital of the Byzantine dominion in Italy.

It was built on the swampy terrain south of the Po delta, but reclamation work over the centuries has given the city dry land and saved its famous monuments, including San Vitale (*below*). This ancient and beautiful Byzantine church, more like a mosque than a Christian church in style, was one of the first centrally planned, domed buildings in the West, consecrated in 547, after the Byzantines had annihilated the Goths. It is

famous both for its mosaics and its apsidal design, which exerted an important influence on the development of western church architecture.

There is an age-old bond between the city and the mouth of the Po (*right*): the waters of the river delta not only acted as a vital and effective defence system in the past but also provided an inexhaustible source of fish and game.

Torrechiara, Emilia Romagna

Torrechiara, in the Apennines near Parma, was built between 1448 and 1480 for the Sforza-Cesarini family. The fifteenth century was the great age of the principalities that ruled the Italian republics, and this splendid and beautiful fortress shows that by that time military architecture was meeting new and different demands: the sophisticated lifestyle at the courts of ruling families put as much emphasis on open terraces as on matters of defence. High walls and machicolations were still indispensable, however, for all the traditional reasons: apart from answering military needs, they were designed to impress the surrounding populace with the might and majesty of the overlord.

Power found its economic resources chiefly in the land, and the castle often dominated miles of countryside and all the people in it, though it did offer protection to the village at its foot.

Bologna, Emilia Romagna

Bologna, the regional capital, is easily identified from the sky: its main streets radiate in a fan shape from either end of a wide central thoroughfare and run out to a series of gates in the old wall that still encircles the city. It grew up on the plan of a Roman military camp, and the present 'old town' dates from the early Middle Ages, before the year 1000.

It is one of Italy's oldest and most beautiful cities, famous for its elegant arcaded streets, its university – the earliest in Europe – its great churches and public buildings, and its towers. In the centre of the picture are the two twelfth-century leaning towers – the Torre degli Asinelli (1119) and the lower Torre Garisenda (begun in 1110) – the best-known of all the buildings of Bologna, relics of the days when powerful families vied with each other for prominence, mounting attacks in times of feud from taller and taller towers; Bologna once had 180.

Ferrara, Emilia Romagna

Ferrara was the rich and splendid seat of the Este dynasty from *c.* 1240 until 1598, and a major centre of Renaissance art and humanism. The Este dukes drew a stream of poets, painters, sculptors and musicians to their illustrious court throughout their reign (Alfonso I, husband of Lucrezia Borgia, was the patron of Titian); they encouraged trade, entertained Petrarch and Pope Eugenius IV, founded a university, laid out new areas of the city and brought Ferrara to a point of supremacy that it held for three centuries.

The cathedral of San Giorgio, whose campanile rises over the heart of the city, mostly dates from the twelfth and thirteenth centuries; the splendid Castello Estense beyond it was constructed as a defensive stronghold in the fourteenth century by Nicolò II d' Este and transformed about two hundred years later into a magnificent ducal palace. This four-square moated fortress, with corner towers and a central courtyard, is one of the finest and best-preserved medieval castles in Italy.

The Centre

*F*lying over central Italy means negotiating the twisting range of the Apennine mountains, but it also means skimming the gentle, civilized hills of Tuscany and Umbria. It allows one to contrast the purplish-blue Tyrrhenian Sea with the ashy-green Adriatic, and – in only a few minutes' flying time – to compare those eternal rivals Florence and Siena, two jewels of central Italy.

From the air the homogeneous landscape of Tuscany, Umbria and northern Lazio becomes a natural fresco. Running the length of central Italy are the rugged mountains of the Apennine chain and stretches of wild and sometimes harsh scrubland, but there are also the softest hills in the world, as one of the characters in Anatole France's *Lys Rouge* remarks: 'What you see is unique in the world. Nowhere else is nature so subtle, elegant and exquisite.' Aldous Huxley, who called Piero della Francesca's *Resurrection* in Sansepolcro, with its background of Tuscan hills, the 'best picture in the world', considered the vast landscape of Umbria and Tuscany, with its qualities of humanity and domesticity, the best of all landscapes for living in.

There is insufficient room in this brief introduction even to mention the names of all the greatest sites in this treasure-house of the Italian peninsula. Rome makes overwhelming demands on one's time and attention; there is something quite overbearing and jealous about Rome, and it could claim all of the limited space available.

Nathaniel Hawthorne, who visited the city in the middle of the nineteenth century, expressed the problems I face in trying to be a narrator in photographs. Hawthorne thought you could leave Rome hating it with all your might and feeling that you would gladly add one more curse to the infinite number that its ancient crimes must have called down upon it. But Hawthorne also remarked on the surprise of discovering that our heartstrings become mysteriously attached to the Eternal City. Rome seems to call us back, as if it were more familiar and more intimately home than the place where we were born. My sentiments exactly.

I am not a Roman. I love Rome, and I detest it. I love it because it has been my home for many years; it is as if I had always lived here. It is equally clear that the amount of time I have lived in Rome is nothing in comparison with the time you would need to know this city. Someone rightly observed that a lifetime is not long enough to do so, and I would not even dare to speak of understanding or explaining it. It may be this very impossibility of ever knowing Rome thoroughly that makes affection give way to disappointment and resentment.

So to make a survey of the city and to examine its history for purely photographic purposes is a daunting task. What is the right angle from which to look at it, and what is the right technique for summing it up in the form of images? When you take to the air and see the whole panorama of the city you realize that there is something breathtaking and infinite about it. It has been called the most historic city of the western world; its influence is impossible to ignore. Culturally it is also the most stratified city on the face of the earth. And this is never so apparent as it is from the sky. From above you can easily distinguish ancient Rome from the medieval and baroque cities, and from that particular complex known as modern Rome.

I have accumulated thousands of different images of the city, and mountains of notes to help me coordinate them. I have had advice from friendly archaeologists, art historians and architects – and from poets too. One day a poet friend gave me a sheet of paper on which he had copied out some lines from the great nineteenth-century Roman poet Giuseppe Giacchino Belli. I kept those lines in my pocket for several months, as a sort of lucky charm. Every now and then I would look at the sheet of paper, read a couple of lines, and hope that my photographs at least partially reflected the living world of the people inside those old buildings in the heart of Rome, the people that Belli immortalized in verse. To quote from him: 'If I should die and be reborn, please God, let me be born again in my Rome . . .'

Urbino, Marche

The fifteenth-century ducal palace of Urbino, a magnificent example of Renaissance architecture, is the masterpiece of Luciano Laurana, who directed the building work from 1465 to 1474.

The house of Montefeltro had ruled the small, isolated town of Urbino, set deep in wild and mountainous country, since the late twelfth century. By the mid-fifteenth century they had acquired a dukedom, and it was the second duke, Federico da Montefeltro, who was Laurana's client. He was an enlightened ruler and a discriminating patron of the arts, and his court was the most dazzling in Italy in its day; the ducal palace itself – the colonnaded courtyards and finely carved stonework, the monumental grand staircase and the duke's own study decorated by Botticelli – reflects Federico's elegant taste and the opulence of the world he inhabited. Built of creamy Dalmation limestone, the palace shines like marble.

Among the many great artists patronized by the house of Montefeltro were Piero della Francesca, Bramante and Raphael, who was born in Urbino.

The palace now houses the Galleria Nazionale delle Marche.

Fiastra, Marche

Near the town of Urbisaglia, south-west of
Macerata, is the famous Cistercian abbey of
Fiastra, built on land given to the order by
the Duke of Spoleto. The abbey was
founded in 1142 and its cloister added
about two hundred years later. What
remains of the original monastic complex
has been skilfully restored.

The culture and learning of the monks
were a great civilizing influence on the
surrounding area, which in those days was
wild and inaccessible.

The Umbrian landscape

The Umbrian Apennines are largely unspoiled, and wild flowers still grow in profusion in the hills and meadows. From early spring until the end of summer poppies and broom add brilliant colour to the landscape. In Umbria, as in other regions of central Italy, the green is sometimes broken by outcrops of stark white chalk, eroded into sharply incised ridges known as *crete (right)*.

Gubbio, Umbria

Gubbio is one of the finest and best-preserved examples of a medieval town in the whole of Italy. Its buildings are spare and muscular, with an air of austerity, but the atmosphere of the place is far from forbidding.

Set on a slope of Monte Ingino in the Apennines, its site is both spectacular and picturesque, an asset of which its architects took full advantage. In the Piazza della Signoria, dramatically raised on high arches, stands the magnificent Palazzo dei Consoli, built in the mid-fourteenth century by Matteo Gattapone. Its stern Romanesque exterior is relieved by delicate arcading in the Gothic style.

The Val di Chiana and Assisi, Umbria

These two aspects of Umbria have much in common: both in the gently sloping fields and vineyards of the Chiana valley and in the medieval town of Assisi a quality of peace exists which has not yet been lost for ever.

Left The lush Val di Chiana stretches from Chiusi to Orvieto. Narrow winding tracks are often the only means of access to secluded valleys, where farming is far from intensive.

Below The tiled roofs of Assisi stretch along the lower slopes of Monte Subasio. The mystical atmosphere of this small city survives in spite of the thousands of tourists and pilgrims who flock here every year. The narrow streets, following the line of the hillside, open out at intervals into beautiful squares: in the Piazza del Comune stands the crenellated Torre Comunale (1275–1305), flanked by the Palazzo del Podestà (1212–82) and the Roman Temple of Minerva, which dates from the first years of the Roman Empire. Just off the far end of the piazza, to the left, is the Oratorio di San Francesco Piccolino, where St Francis was born, and at the farthest end of the town stands the great basilica dedicated to his memory.

Maremma, Tuscany

The last surviving marshes of Maremma, south of Grosseto: this swampland region, ravaged by malaria throughout the Middle Ages, once extended for hundreds of miles along the Tyrrhenian coast, from a little way south of Livorno to Civitavecchia in Lazio. Drainage schemes, started by the Etruscans and continued by medieval monks, were completed only between 1930 and 1960, when malaria was finally eradicated. The marshes are now reduced to a few protected areas like those around the town of Orbetello, and the buffaloes and half-wild horses that were once numerous have almost entirely disappeared. Orbetello clings to a narrow strip of land in the middle of a lagoon: originally an Etruscan colony, it was fortified by the Spanish in 1557. Today it is being swallowed up by the fashionable Costa Argenta.

In the distance is the Argentario promontory, which acts as a barrier between the marshes and the Tyrrhenian Sea.

Montecristo, Tuscany

The wild and desolate island of Montecristo rises from the Tyrrhenian Sea between the Italian coast and Corsica, with its jagged granite peak known as Monte Fortezza more than two thousand feet above sea level. The island was once the hunting reserve of the Savoy kings, and has recently been declared a nature reserve.

So seriously does the local government take its duties to protect the wildlife that visitors are allowed no further than the cove where boats dock on day trips from Elba.

Lucca, Tuscany (left)

Lucca's small elliptical Piazza del Mercato was built on the ruins of the amphitheatre of the original Roman town. Narrow streets lined with medieval houses lead round the square to the twelfth-century church of San Frediano, whose tall Romanesque tower is a landmark in this northern section of the city. To the far left, on the site of the Roman forum, is the church of San Michele in Foro, begun in Lucca's heyday at the height of the Middle Ages.

Before the rise of Florence and Pisa Lucca was the most important commune in Tuscany, with an economy based on banking and the manufacture of gold-leaf and silk brocades. But feuds between Guelphs and Ghibellines, and the rivalry of up-and-coming Florence, had put Lucca in the shade by the fourteenth century, and though it had periods of revival it never quite recovered its early pre-eminence. Now its greatest claim to fame is its superb olive oil.

Pisa, Tuscany (above)

The Piazza dei Miracoli in Pisa is more impressive than anything prepares one to expect – especially when seen from the air. The Cathedral, the Leaning Tower, the Baptistery and the Camposanto, all in white marble and set against the green of the square, have an impact that is breathtaking.

The Cathedral was begun in 1063 and work continued into the thirteenth century, with later additions and alterations, but it is marked by a rare unity of style. The cylindrical campanile or Leaning Tower also took a long time to complete (1173–1350): subsidence caused the building to lean and interrupted work for a hundred years. Attempts were made to correct the inclination when building resumed, and today the tower is safe from further subsidence – cement has been injected to support it – though it still leans nearly fifteen feet out of the perpendicular. The Baptistery, a magnificent circular building, was begun in 1152; its Gothic dome and pointed arches were added in the fourteenth century. Behind the three main monuments is the Camposanto, a long, rectangular cemetery in the form of an enclosed cloister lit by beautiful traceried windows. By the time it was finished, in the fifteenth century, the Piazza dei Miracoli had become one of the great marvels of Pisan Romanesque architecture.

Florence and its landscape, Tuscany

Opposite Etruscan and Roman settlements existed here before the rise of medieval Florence, which was flourishing by about 1000. In the later Middle Ages and High Renaissance, with the work of Dante, Giotto, Donatello, Leonardo and Michelangelo – all of them Florentine – this unique city reached its zenith. Its streets are still lined with the *palazzi* of great Florentine families, and its museums and churches overflow with the work of painters and sculptors whom they patronized. The Cathedral of Florence – with Brunelleschi's dome and Giotto's Campanile – and the octagonal Baptistery in front of it form the nucleus of the old city, which extends to the great church of Santa Croce (its spectacular white façade can be seen in the background), and on to the banks of the Arno river.

Left Aldous Huxley considered the hills around Florence to be the sweetest landscape in the world. They owe their preservation to their inhabitants rather than to environmental legislation, and their gentle serenity is the perfect complement to the splendour of the regional capital. Winding country roads lead past stone farmhouses with small round haystacks, through olive and cypress groves, and up to scattered hilltop villages where the air is cooler than in the city at the height of summer.

Monti dell'Uccellina, Tuscany

Monti dell'Uccellina, near Grosseto, has
been a national park since 1977; just as
Montecristo remained unspoiled because it
was once the private property of the Savoy
kings, so these forests and deserted beaches
have survived unaltered because the entire
coast and the hills behind it were once the
preserve of the Grand Dukes of Tuscany.
Nowadays the regional and central
government alike forbid any building in the
area.

The shells of a number of ancient guard
towers, and the romantic remains of the
twelfth-century abbey of San Rabano, can
still be seen along this isolated stretch. One
of the most striking landmarks is the Torre
della Bella Marsilia, the lonely remnant of
the castle of Collecchio. In 1543 the castle
was destroyed by Barbarossa and all its
occupants murdered – except for the
beautiful Margherita, who was swept off to
the harem of Suleiman the Magnificent,
there to become his legitimate sultana.

77

Siena, Tuscany

Mellow terracotta tiles, some used to make
improvized repairs in irregular patterns,
lead the eye over the roofs of Siena to the
Piazza del Campo, the focal point of the
city. This is the scene of the *Palio,* the
spectacular annual horse race dating from
the Middle Ages, which demonstrates a
fierce pride on the part of its citizens that
has long outlived Siena's early days of
power and artistic brilliance.

The Campo, shaped like a scallop shell,
occupies the site of the Roman forum.
Among the beautiful brick buildings around
it the most famous are the austere Palazzo
Pubblico (1297–1310) and its neighbouring
tower, the Torre del Mangia (1338–48)
which rises to a height of 296 feet – a
daring architectural venture for its day, and
considered so foolhardy that its builders, the
Rinaldo brothers, were required to bear the
entire risk themselves. Opposite is the wide,
curved façade of the Palazzo Sansedoni, one
of the most striking palaces on the square.

Second only to Florence, always its rival,
as a Tuscan treasure-house of art and
architecture, Siena rose to its greatest
heights in the thirteenth and fourteenth
centuries, when it produced painters such as
Duccio, Simone Martini, and Ambrogio and
Pietro Lorinzetti, all of whose work can still
be seen here.

Bagnoregio, Lazio

This little town lies east of Lake Bolsena, high on its own small plateau of volcanic tufa. The site was first settled in Etruscan times, over 2,500 years ago, and its natural defences made it almost unassailable.

For the past century, however, this very advantage has become the cause of its decline. The tufa ridge has been crumbling away year by year, drastically reducing the habitable area, and the population has now shrunk to a few dozen people.

The Ponte Abadía, Lazio (right)

The little Fiora river runs west to the sea, almost at the boundary of Lazio with Tuscany. For the Etruscans it was an important link between the Tyrrhenian Sea and the interior.

In the sixth century BC they built a bridge over the river, spanning a narrow ravine, and the Romans later enlarged it to carry the Via Aurelia. The foundations of this beautiful bridge, known as the Ponte Abadía, have survived since Etruscan times; its arch is Roman. In the twelfth century a castle was built beside it, strategically placed to block, with a single garrison, the road north to Rome, the city of the Popes.

Villages of Lazio

(Left) Capodimonte, a picturesque little
village on the edge of Lake Bolsena in
northern Lazio. The lake, whose clean, clear
water is full of fish, occupies a large and
ancient crater; it has no large towns around
it, and the lush green farmland, woods and
gardens on its banks are typical of much of
the land north and east of Rome in being
richly productive. As a result, villages and
hamlets have taken over every farmable
space. One of the most unusual is San
Gregorio da Sàssola (*above right*). It dates
from the eighteenth century, when a little
village on the site was razed in order to
rebuild it in a more convenient form for the
communal life of a group of farming
families.

Rome, Lazio

A general view of Rome in a photograph
taken three hundred feet above the
Capitoline Hill: in the centre is the vast
white bulk of the monument to Victor
Emmanuel II, with Michelangelo's
Campidoglio (its square has a distinctive
circular design) a little nearer the camera;
beyond the monument are Trajan's Forum
and the tall white shaft of Trajan's Column,
with the semi-circular building known as
Trajan's Market and the Forum of Augustus
to the right; to the right again lies the
so-called Roman Forum. These open spaces,
which served largely as centres for public
discussion, occupy the level plain between
the Capitoline and Palatine hills, two of the
seven hills on which ancient Rome was
built.

   The city is said to have been founded by
Romulus and Remus in 734 BC, but there
was a Latin settlement on the Capitoline, on
the left bank of the Tiber, as early as 1000
BC. The Roman republic grew up on social
and physical foundations laid down by the
Etruscans, and in the course of the next
seven centuries, helped by successes in the
Punic Wars, it reached its Golden Age, built
great monuments, expanded its dominion
and became the first city of world stature.
By the second century AD it had a
population of over a million. At its greatest
extent the empire that it founded stretched
from Scotland to the Sahara and from the
Strait of Gibraltar to the Persian Gulf, and
the civilization it produced, a synthesis of all
the cultures of the ancient world, is the basis
of western life and civilization today.

The Vatican City

The first church on the site of the Vatican was built by Constantine the Great in 324. The present one, a monumental creation designed principally by Bramante, Raphael and Michelangelo, is one of the greatest architectural works of the Renaissance. Two wide semi-circular colonnades, the inspiration and masterpiece of Bernini, enclose St Peter's Square; crowning them are 140 gigantic statues of saints and martyrs set there as vigilant protectors of the Catholic faith, the guards of the Church of Rome.

All this architectural and theatrical grandeur, designed to astound and overwhelm, was intended as an instrument of propaganda. The word is accurate since it was first used by De Propaganda Fide, the institute created by the popes to serve as the highest authority of the Catholic Church, and to protect and promote its interests *ad majorem Deo gloriam* (to the greater glory of God). The instructions given to Bernini in commissioning the design of the square and colonnade are still preserved in the Vatican Library: 'Since the Church of St Peter is the mother of all the other churches . . . let it have a portico able to receive her pilgrims in its wide open arms . . .'

87

Anguillara Sabazia, Lazio

Like many of Lazio's lakes, Bracciano, north-west of Rome – an almost perfect circle of deep blue water – occupies the crater of an extinct volcano, and rolling green hills and farmland sweep gently down to its wooded shoreline. In Etruscan times a settlement was established here, the site of present-day Anguillara Sabazia, on the small promontory that protrudes into the water on its south-eastern side. The town probably takes its name from the Italian word for eel, *anguilla*; the lake is full of eels, particularly at its mouth behind the promontory, and Anguillara is famous for them.

Two faces of Abruzzo

Until very recently time seemed to have stood still in Abruzzo, contained in valleys cut off between high mountains: life was immutable – a pastoral, inward-looking existence still focused on religion and monastic communities.

The delightful Abbey of San Clemente a Casàuria (*above*), a simple Romanesque building near the village of Torre de' Pàsseri, was founded in 871 by the Emperor Lodovico II, and rebuilt by the Cistercians in the twelfth century (its original crypt still survives). The façade has a fine arcaded portico with an upper storey added in 1448.

But some peaceful backwaters are changing dramatically to keep pace with the new industrialized Italy. A symbol of modern Abruzzo is the Telespazio – Italy's space communications centre (*opposite*), which grew up on the site of former Lake Fucino, east of Avezzano, in the 1960s.

Though the buildings are recent, the draining of the lake was first attempted in AD 52, when the Emperor Claudius dug a tunnel to connect the lake to the basin of the Liri river. Unfortunately, his efforts met with little success. Frederick II tried to reopen the tunnel in 1240, but it was not until 1852 that work began again in earnest. The old route was followed more or less and the new tunnel was opened in 1875. This time the scheme worked: the outflow is used by electrical installations at Capistrello, to the south-west.

In 1951 the land reclaimed from the lake, which formed part of the estate of a wealthy Roman family, was expropriated and about 35,000 acres divided among 8,000 families.

The ancient Abruzzo

These images of Abruzzo, separated by about fifteen hundred years, are expressions of two very different civilizations that have left their mark on the Apennines.

The ruins of Alba Fucens (*above*), the chief Roman stronghold in the uplands of central Italy, once housed 6,000 people and extended over three hills. Excavations have revealed stretches of the ancient Via Valeria, the main street of the town, as well as a forum, a basilica, a market, shops and houses, a theatre, public baths and an amphitheatre.

Celano (*right*) is one of the most splendid of all the Abruzzo castles. Begun in 1392 and completed in 1463, it was built on a courtyard plan, with four square towers and projecting battlements. The mullioned windows were added in the fifteenth century, perhaps by Antonio Piccolomini, a descendant of the castle's original builder. The central court is encircled by a Gothic colonnade and an open gallery, with round arches and columns bearing the Piccolomini seal on the capitals. The castle is surrounded by a polygonal curtain wall fortified with square bastions along the ramparts and cylindrical towers at the corners.

Sulmona, Abruzzo

Under the shadow of the medieval aqueduct
the square in Sulmona, one of the few towns
in a sparsely populated area, is packed with
an Easter Sunday crowd. People from miles
around converge here to celebrate Easter,
which is a major feastday throughout the
region.

These devout believers also preserve a
faith in pre-Christian rites such as the spring
festival: the significance of Easter, often the
first opportunity to get together after a long,
hard winter, is inseparable here from the
real and symbolic importance of the coming
of spring and from the ancient traditions
associated with it.

The climate in Abruzzo's wild bare
mountains is harsh in both summer and
winter, with snow lying for months on the
higher peaks. Until comparatively recently
there were few roads, and remote valleys
were often accessible only on foot; even
now a village might be cut off for weeks
during a spell of bad weather.

Pesche, Abruzzo

Pesche, an austere and isolated town in the central Apennines, is all but deserted today, and in that it illustrates a common phenomenon: a host of small towns and hilltop villages have been abandoned in the relatively recent past, and doors and windows stand open. Statistics indicate that more than 250,000 people have left the Abruzzo region in the last thirty years, and the population of the central Apennines as a whole has been decimated over the past few centuries.

The first major causes were the terrible earthquakes and plagues of the seventeenth century. The second involved all of southern and central Italy in the early twentieth century, and resulted from epidemics of phylloxera that devastated the vineyards and dealt a mortal blow to the peasant economy. Thousands left for America in the decades between the wars. The last exodus has been in progress since 1945, partly in the direction of Rome, partly towards northern Europe (Germany and Belgium in particular), and increasingly towards Canada and Australia.

But there is also a movement in the opposite direction. These remote, seemingly romantic little towns, attract increasing numbers of visitors. The Abruzzo national park, the Rocche highlands and the Cinque Miglia plateau, as well as villages like Pesche which seemed abandoned forever, now act as a draw for tourism which may lead to a rebirth of the region.

Duronia, Molise

The little farming village of Duronia lies to the east of Pesche in Molise, a region only recently separated from Abruzzo.

In the sixth to seventh century BC this area was the home of the Samnites, a tough Italic people whom the legions of Rome had a hard time suppressing.

Archaeological research has shown that the layout of Duronia closely follows that of Samnite settlements, and from the air the fields of the Molise Apennines can be seen to follow ancient Samnite agricultural patterns. Even the names of people living here in the first millennium BC have survived, despite recent population shifts, and Marsi, Aequi, Paeligni, Vestini and Marruccini are all local names today. Until the end of the last century people lived in isolation in this inhospitable landscape, cut off from each other by mountain ridges, with little opportunity of exchange with the world outside.

The South

The route of our third flight takes us over the most Mediterranean regions of the Italian peninsula and the islands of Sicily and Sardinia. There is nothing better than a sky-high view to grasp the sense of a land that protrudes into the very heart of the Mediterranean.

The coast of Italy's 'deep south' has remained all but uncontaminated by destructive transformation and building, and the waters of its rocky bays and inlets are almost magically translucent, the clearest (with a few exceptions) of the entire peninsula. Along this southern coast we can mark one by one those shoreline sites to east, west and south that saw the arrival of colonists, immigrants, raiders, liberators, speculators and tourists. We can trace the routes inland from the sea that were followed by successive waves of invaders whose conquests so influenced for better and for worse the whole southern region of Italy.

The helicopter takes us along stretches of the Sicilian coast that are glowing and untouched, like the area reaching from Avola, south of Siracuse, to Cape Passero, the southernmost tip, and north-west almost all the way to Gela. At Cape Vaticano in Calabria, facing west to the Lipari islands, sheer cliffs rise vertically from the shore, deterring any attempt to make a landing, but in many other parts of Calabria and Basilicata we skim over the tops of reed thickets at small river mouths. These narrow watercourses marked the first main lines followed by newcomers from the sea as they turned towards the interior. Along these uncontaminated coasts we can let our imagination run free: it is easy to suppose that we can see the dark shadows left on the sands by boats hauled up on the shore by Greeks, Phoenicians, Arabs and Spaniards, or, in recent times, by the Allied landing craft that touched ground in the south of Italy at the start of the liberation of Europe.

But our trip brings real shapes into view as well as imaginary ones as we fly over the fashionable beaches of southern Italy, the crowded haunts of day trippers and the exclusive havens of the rich. Here a wake has been left in the sea by the latest peaceful invasion of the Italian coast, the invasion of tourist steamers, luxury yachts, rubber dinghies and plastic speeedboats. The streams of people who have come to southern Italy over the sea still continues.

The first to come from the eastern shores of the Mediterranean were the Greeks, followed by the Byzantines. The Punic Phoenicians and then the Arabs made their approach from the southern Mediterranean. And the Allies were not the first to come from the west: that was the direction that Nelson came from at the end of the eighteenth century. So did the Bourbon ships, and Garibaldi with his thousand Red Shirts.

These coastal landings obviously had major repercussions, establishing relationships with the interior of the country that may not be as apparent from the ground as they are from the sky. From above it is easy to trace the physical geography and the geological demarcations that have established natural lines of communication between coast and interior as well as the course of cultural transmission.

You could not, for example, understand the purpose of Frederick II's Castel del Monte, standing high over the Puglian plain, without taking account, as you do from the air, of the nearby ports – Molfetta and Trani, among others – where the Crusader ships set sail for the Holy Land. Nor could you fully grasp the historical significance of the cathedral that dominates Cefalú in Sicily without understanding its earlier form – it used to be a mosque, and its original plan is clearly visible from the sky.

The Arabs built the mosque in the ninth century, as soon as they brought their feluccas ashore. This may seem remote in time, dating back more than a thousand years, but over a thousand years earlier, other people had come from Greece to conquer this fertile peninsula jutting into the middle of the Mediterranean. They were to leave the most enduring impression on the history of southern Italy, which they called Enotria. The Magna Graecia they created decisively influenced the subsequent development of the civilization of Italy and continued to do so until recent times.

If we turn the helicopter over the Ionian Sea and head due west, towards the point where the sun sets behind the shores and mountains of Basilicata, Calabria and Sicily, our route will be exactly the one followed by the first Greek settlers as they headed towards their new homeland.

Flying south over the shores of Basilicata and Calabria, down the Ionian coast and along the Sicilian shore, we can see several sites still famous today for those first Greek landings – Crotone, Megara Hyblea, Sybaris, Naxos. These and other places along the coast saw the landing of Greek colonists in the eighth century BC, settlers guided by the chronicles of their oral tradition, which were partly mythical and partly true. These chronicles related the experiences of explorers who had landed centuries earlier, and told of the advantages and perils of the 'new places' in the west, of the Enotria of legend and reality.

Obviously there are no visible traces of the first landings of those explorers, nor of the first colonists. How could there be? But if you look down from the sky you can understand the choices they made in terms of landing site, beach, gulf or promontory.

In the course of many years I have had several occasions to fly over the area where the Greeks landed on the coast at Megara Hyblea, not far from Siracuse in Sicily. A French archaeological mission under the direction of Professor Vallet has been working for some time to bring to light the successive levels of construction that document the increasingly complex settlements of the Greek colonists from the seventh century BC onwards. They have traced their development from the first, clearly identifiable house to the establishment of a genuine urban nucleus.

Without flying over Megara Hyblea in a helicopter, I do not think I would ever have realized how physically close the coastal zone settled and urbanized by the Greeks was to the mountains inhabited by the indigenous Italic peoples all those centuries ago: two immediately adjacent worlds, but separated by barriers of suspicion and hostility. At the same time they were mutually attracted by a desire for exchange and contact, essential to their growth and development.

Nowadays these two ancient areas of settlement are linked by autostradas and

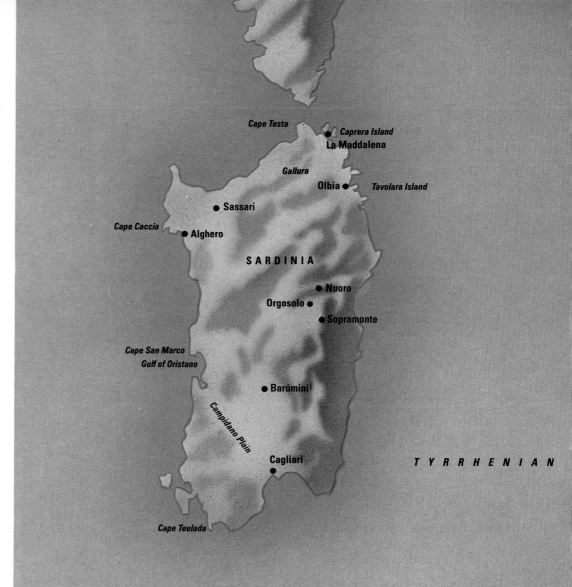

Cape Testa
Caprera Island
La Maddalena
Gallura
Olbia
Tavolara Island
Sassari
Cape Caccia
Alghero
SARDINIA
Nuoro
Orgosolo
Sopramonte
Cape San Marco
Gulf of Oristano
Barúmini
Campidano Plain
Cagliari
TYRRHENIAN

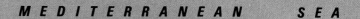

MEDITERRANEAN   SEA

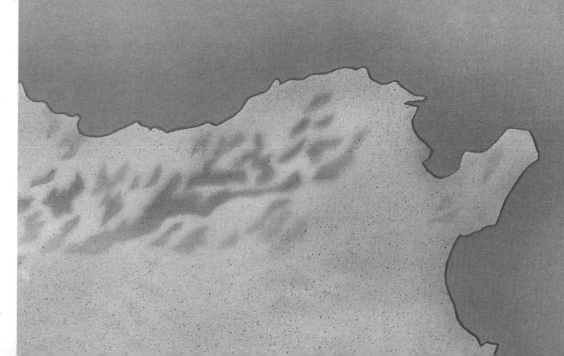

SICILY
Pantelleria
MALTA
TUNISIA
Lampedusa

APENNINES

Lake Varano

PUGLIA

Margherita di Savoìa
Trani

CAMPANIA

Molfetta
Bari

Casertavecchia

Castel del Monte
Polignano a Mare

Gulf of Gaeta

River Volturne

Altavilla Irpina

Valle del
Sabato

Alberobello
Ostuni

Naples

Castel di Lagopesole

Brindisi

Mount Vesuvius

Herculaneum

Matera

Martina Franca

Pròcida

Pompeii

River Bradano

Ischia

Potenza

Sant'Angelo

Gulf of Naples

Salerno

Taranto

BASILICATA

Capri

Gulf of Salerno

River Basento

Paestum

Cilento

River Agri

Elea

Sapri

Rivello

Sibari

River Crati

Rossano

LA SILA

SEA

CALABRIA

Crotone

Le Castella

Tropea

IONIAN

Cape Vaticano

SEA

Lipari Islands

Strait of
Messina

Naxos

Reggio di Calabria

Palermo

Egadi Islands

Trápani

Formica

Cefalù

Segesta

Motya

Marsala

Mount Etna

SICILY

Aci Trezza

Catania

Agrigento

Gela

Megara Hyblea

Syracuse

Ragusa

Avola

Cape Passero

MALTA

overrun by factories, hotels and dense urban agglomerations of reinforced concrete apartment blocks. In the past, those few intervening miles were a kind of no-man's-land, where generation after generation the 'civilized' Greeks and the Italic 'savages' came together in encounter and conflict. (Indeed, these 'primitives' became increasingly evolved and culturally advanced just because of that difficult but fruitful contact.)

That particular relationship existed in a hundred other sites throughout Magna Graecia. In some of them not a trace of their distant past has survived while in others impressive remains are still visible, especially from the sky.

Hundreds of medieval towers can be seen from the helicopter along the inhabited shores and in the most isolated regions of southern Italy, where almost everywhere the mountains run right down to the sea, forming promontories that are accessible only on foot or by boat or helicopter. These towers stood guard over southern Italy against the Saracen menace. Warning signals were passed from tower to tower on sighting pirates without a flag, or marauders who flaunted theirs, the green banner of the prophet Mohammed. Today they survive as a striking and unmistakable feature of the southern coasts.

There is one tower, much like all the others, a powerful crenellated structure which dominates Cape San Marco, the northern promontory enclosing the Gulf of Oristano in western Sardinia. This is the site of the ruins of the Phoenician settlement of Tharros. The sea that washes the west coast of Sardinia is almost always corrugated by the mistral, and our helicopter trembled and bounced in the wind. Cape San Marco seems to emerge like a long-stalked mushroom from the Sardinian coast, which is flat and sandy in this region. The promontory is almost an island with only a slender isthmus joining it to the shore, and seems inaccessible from the land. Indeed the isthmus is so narrow that the site was easy to defend when the Phoenician trading settlement was attacked by the indigenous population, the warlike Sardinian tribes of the area.

The native population of Sardinia, like the Sicani in Sicily and other Italic peoples on the mainland, defended themselves against invasion from the sea, and they often passed to the attack. But in Sardinia, as well as elsewhere, they did not reject contact and interchange as well. In contrast with the indigenous peoples of peninsular Italy, the Sardinians traded with people who came from the sea, but they did not neglect to fortify the interior of their island. Generation after generation added to the chain of *nuraghi* (fortified settlements) that are still visible as a powerful line of defence. The *nuraghi* mark out a geographically uncertain border that is clearly visible from the sky, a line that then separated two races and two cultures, a foreign culture along the shore and a native one inland.

Here too a flight along the coast helps us to understand the interior of the region. It is an aid not only in reaching back into the past to find the roots of the Mediterranean civilization of the peninsula, but also in understanding the relationship between coast and interior in modern times. And it helps to make sense of the population shift that has marked the urban development of all regions of southern Italy.

Fly over Campania, Calabria, Sicily and Sardinia and you will see how few and far between are the urban centres along the shore. There are, of course, a few coastal cities that have always been major seaports, but in southern Italy more than seventy per cent of the 'coastal' towns stand several miles inland. They are almost always on hilltops, in conformity with a settlement tradition that is deep-rooted throughout the Mediterranean and based on an instinctive fear of the threat that comes from the sea.

Nowadays the invasion is solely that of tourists, and the harm is therefore only ecological. But in the past, when the foreigner was also a predator, the conflict was always with an enemy who came ashore to attack. There is one exception, and that is Puglia: the Puglian coast is lined with ports, some of them very small. This is because there was a migratory movement in the opposite direction as well, a movement from the coast to the sea. I am referring to the Crusaders, whose main embarkation points were the ports of Puglia. It was from here that they left the shores of Christendom; it was here that their ships hoisted anchor on their departure to the infidel east, unfurling enormous sails in the shadow of towering Romanesque cathedrals built on the very brink of the sea. The marvellous cathedral of Trani deserves special mention: viewed from a helicopter, it looks like a gigantic stage set against the limitless perspective of the sea.

The Crusaders were part of that long procession of armies, colonists and 'liberators' who turned southern Italy into a field thick with crosses and marked indelibly by self-interested attempts to 'free' the south from the domination of others. The Byzantines came to southern Italy to save the peninsula from the Barbarians in the sixth, seventh and eighth centuries; the Normans came to drive out the Arabs in the eleventh century; the Red Shirts of Garibaldi came in the nineteenth century to break the bonds of Bourbon rule. And it was at Marsala in Sicily that the Moslem invaders made their landing. It was actually they who named the site Marsa-Allah ('Port of Allah').

You cannot mention Garibaldi's Red Shirts in a chapter about southern Italy without mentioning the bay of Marsala, where they came ashore. This, of course, was not just another episode in the history of invasions, landings and colonization of the Italian coast, but a high point in the history of Italy, a moment of glory.

There are a host of places in the Mediterranean which interweave conflicting feelings, wonderment at their beauty and melancholy at the events that occurred there. Flying among the majestic rocks of Cape Palinuro, not far from Sapri, one's thoughts turn to the unfortunate Palinurus, Aeneas's helmsman. This is where he is said to have fallen into the sea and drowned. Looking down a luminous stretch of white sand between sheer rock walls I discovered the small secret inlet where Aeneas cremated the body of his friend and named the site after him. It looks like a corner of paradise, but it was a place of death and sorrow.

What recollections remain after a long and tortuous flight over such a complex area as southern Italy? They are as many and as varied as the tesserae in a mosaic and they crowd the memory like a firework display, full of baroque extravaganzas and volcanic flames.

Altavilla Irpina, Campania

This village in the Sabato river valley is one
of a host of small medieval hilltowns
scattered over Campania, between the sea to
the west and the Apennines to the east.

The region is one of the oldest, most
fertile and well irrigated farming areas of
the Italian peninsula. In medieval times it
was also very violent: its land and
communities were frequently plundered,
with the result that each small town built a
watchtower to keep a lookout for raiders.
The tower had to be strong enough to
withstand long sieges and large enough to
protect all the inhabitants of the settlement
who sought refuge within its walls.

Like so many small country towns and
villages, Altavilla Irpina was built high up
not only to make use of the strategic
advantages of a hilltop site but also, and
perhaps more importantly, to leave the
fertile land in the valley free for cultivation.

The Bay of Naples, Campania

The Castel dell'Ovo, on the ancient island of Megaris, was begun in 1154 for William I, continued under Frederick II and restored by the Anjou rulers as a royal palace; behind it Mount Vesuvius looms high over the Bay of Naples, its snow-capped summit lost in cloud. Its name derives from two roots meaning 'the unextinguished': the last eruption of Vesuvius occurred in 1944. It is the only active volcano on the continent of Europe.

This was the scene, once framed by tall pines and perfumed gardens, that inspired the saying, 'See Naples and die'. Sadly, the expression seems to have changed its significance in recent years: the city and its bay are both being steadily ruined by pollution and development. Since the last war industrial and residential suburbs have spread in all directions round the bay, eating up its shoreline and irreversibly damaging an area that has always been considered one of the great beauty spots of the world.

Pròcida, Campania

On the island of Pròcida in the Bay of Naples, between Ischia and the mainland, a castle, now a prison, towers on a precipitous crag of volcanic rock. A strategically important fortress in its day, the castle was occupied three times by the British Navy during wars with the French, in 1799, 1806 and 1813. It was in 1799 that the revolutionary Admiral Francesco Caracciolo is said to have been hanged from the yardarm of his flagship in the Bay of Naples.

Pompeii, Campania

When Vesuvius erupted in AD 79 Pompeii and the surrounding countryside were buried under some twenty-three feet of cinder, ash and lapilli.

Painstaking excavation of the town has continued since the eighteenth century, and now provides the basis of our knowledge of domestic life in ancient times. So far sixty per cent of the ruins have been uncovered. The remains of the forum, the religious, political and economic heart of the city – the equivalent of a main square – can be seen in the centre of the picture; its broad rectangular space was surrounded by a colonnade with a gallery above it for spectators of the games held here before the amphitheatre was built. In the foreground, at right angles to the forum, are the remains of the basilica, and in the angle formed by these two buildings is the Temple of Apollo. The Via dell'Abbondanza runs away into the distance, lined with mansions, villas and public offices. The town had a population of about twenty thousand and was exclusively a commerical centre. The ruins are so extensive and varied that they offer a real insight into the beliefs and activities of the inhabitants, their trading practices, building methods, and all manner of different aspects of private and public life.

Herculaneum, Campania

Said to have been founded by Hercules and named after him, Herculaneum was a largely residential seaside town until the eruption of Vesuvius. Unlike Pompeii, with its population of middle-class merchants, it had a mixed society of artisans, fishermen and rich patricians, the aristocrats of ancient Rome. Judging from its variety of architecture and rich, sophisticated decoration, it was artistically freer and more evolved than Pompeii. Another vital difference between them is that while Pompeii was destroyed by the heat and weight of tons of ash and cinders, a sea of mud and molten lava buried Herculaneum, seeping deep into every crack and crevice and setting rock hard, shutting out the air and preserving the contents of many of its buildings almost intact. As a result, excavations have brought to light a wealth of detailed information – exquisite frescoes, personal belongings, even the bodies of the people themselves.

This group of houses facing a row of columns, which probably supported a tiled canopy over the street, still stands two storeys high. It came to light in digs carried out between 1828 and 1875. A massive amount of work has been done since the first discoveries were made in 1709, but much of the city and its treasures will probably never be revealed.

Ischia, Campania

This sort of image inspired the scholar and historian Fernand Braudel to describe the Mediterranean as 'a sea of mountains'. The spur of Punta Sant'Angelo juts out into the Tyrrhenian Sea on the south side of Ischia, the first place the Greeks settled in Italy, in the eighth century BC.

Ischia is volcanic and very fertile – a delicious white wine is produced on the slopes of the extinct Mount Epomeo – and hot radioactive mineral springs bubble out of the ground in a number of places; there are some around Punta Sant'Angelo. Today Ischia is following overcrowded Capri as an international tourist island, but so far this rocky peninsula is safe from high-rise flats and huge hotels.

Casertavecchia, Campania

The view from the air of this little town, a few miles north of Naples, captures the atmosphere and unity of its picturesque jumble of ancient buildings. It was founded in the eighth century by the Lombards of Capua. The splendid Romanesque cathedral of San Michele dates from 1113–53, with a campanile of a century later and an octagonal lantern under a round, tiled cap, decorated in a wonderfully effective blend of Sicilian and Byzantine styles.

The town has been largely depopulated over the last hundred and fifty years so little has been done to alter its character – there is not a television aerial to be seen. But many of the old houses are now derelict and roofs are beginning to fall in as the old town is deserted in favour of new Caserta.

Rivello, Basilicata

The harmony of style and colouring of the small town of Rivello, east of Sapri, is typical of the hilltowns around the Campania-Basilicata border.

A medieval castle overlooks the surrounding territory from a vantage point on rising ground while the houses cling tightly together along the ridge. The town seems perfectly moulded to the contours of the hill, and the houses well adapted to the steeply sloping site: the side facing down the valley is often two or three storeys higher than the side backing on to the hill.

The Basento valley, Basilicata (right)

The vast estates of the days of feudalism represented an imbalance of wealth and power that is largely responsible for the economic state of southern Italy today. But much of the south suffers from an economic failure of another sort, based on complex divisions of land between families over many generations. According to tradition, farmland is parcelled out in small patches, impeding rationalization and the introduction of mechanization. Change has been a long time coming, but it is on the way in some areas: old divisions between small plots have been swept away in this part of the Basento valley, making broad stretches of arable land that can be run much more profitably than in the past.

Matera, Basilicata

The Romanesque cathedral (1268–70) rises high above the city of Matera, an extraordinary and extremely ancient settlement built on a precipice overlooking the gorge of the river Gravina.

There are traces of Palaeolithic villages nearby, and the site of the town itself was occupied by Pyrrhus and Hannibal. Sacked by the Goths, it was taken in turn by the Lombards, the Franks and the Saracens. Driven out by imperial troops, the Saracens reoccupied the town in 937 and finally destroyed it completely in 944, when they killed all its male inhabitants and enslaved its women. In the early eleventh century, under the rule of Byzantium, Matera was rebuilt, but its long history of oppression and devastation had by then driven its citizens away; they took to the caves carved in the rock faces and ravines beneath the town. These so-called *sassi*, or rock dwellings, are a disturbingly evocative testimony to Matera's past. The modern town, though expanding, is still poor and suffers many of the complex and painful problems that dominate the south.

Matera, Basilicata

At the foot of the gorge overlooked by
Matera are the poorest of the *sassi*, the cave
dwellings below the town. Until
comparatively recently half Matera's
population of nearly 50,000 lived in these
terraced caves on either side of the ravine.
The *sassi* have no windows, only doors
open to let in light and air. Entire families
and their animals – men, women, children,
sheep, goats, dogs and pigs – slept together
in these dark holes, infested with flies and
disease; the death rate among children born
in the *sassi* was nearly forty-five per cent.
The peasants and their children walked long
distances to work in the fields, and it was
only on Sundays that these 'outsiders'
entered the city proper, when they went to
the cathedral for mass.

Until a few years ago people still lived in
the *sassi* and eked out an existence
somehow, despite efforts to move them to
ugly modern flats nearby.

Castel di Lagopésole, Basilicata

Lagopésole, north of Potenza, was built by Emperor Frederick II of Hohenstaufen in 1242; it was the last and the largest of all his great southern Italian fortresses. Their speed of construction was astonishing given the technology of the time and the backwardness of the area. Unlike Frederick's other castles, Lagopésole was laid out on a rectangular plan with two inner courtyards, and was designed as a hunting lodge at a time when the land around was wooded and full of game. It was one of the Emperor's favourite residences, and he spent the last summer of his life here.

Buildings of Puglia

Above The finest Italian castle built by Emperor Frederick II of Hohenstaufen is the Castel del Monte, a masterpiece of its kind. Built around 1240, of golden limestone, it was laid out on an octagonal plan round a central courtyard. It has been suggested that Frederick II designed it himself and that he chose an octagon to represent the eight-sided crown of the Holy Roman Empire.

The area known as the Murge, in which it stands, was then a dense forest and the castle was used as a hunting lodge. Its interior fittings were extremely sophisticated for their day and included among other things a plumbing system.

Ironically, after the defeat of the Hohenstaufens by the house of Anjou in 1268, the castle was used as a prison for Frederick II's grandchildren who were locked up here for thirty years.

By the mid-nineteenth century the castle had become the haunt of brigands and a shelter for shepherds, but it was rescued from dereliction by the State in 1876 and has been restored as a national monument.

Right Stretching into the far horizon, the flat mosaic of fields around Alberobello is dotted with the strange mushroom-shaped houses known as *trulli* that are unique to the area.

Their conical roofs were originally built of wood and straw, later replaced by stone, each tile jutting above the one underneath without mortar between. It is thought that their style of construction was devised by feudal landlords so that a rope could be fastened to the pommel on the roof and the house pulled down if the peasants failed to pay their taxes.

Two towns in Puglia

The dazzling white town of Ostuni (*left*) is built on three hills and dates from pre-Roman times. Steep medieval streets, lined with houses that look more African than European, climb up to the heart of the old quarter and the great cathedral (1435–60), which combines Gothic and Venetian influences in its beautiful exterior.

Martina Franca (*below*) is overlooked by the collegiate church of San Martino, a graceful eighteenth-century building, unmistakably baroque in style. Over the doorway is a representation of St Martin and the beggar. The town was established in the tenth century by refugees from Táranto who were forced inland by the Saracen invasion.

In style these two towns have much in common, and their vernacular architecture has changed very little with the passage of time. The houses follow complex, labyrinthine plans that are probably Islamic in origin, and they are separated by tiny squares and alleyways that wind through the towns like a maze, often coming to an abrupt and unexpected halt. In Martina Franca a hundred and sixty blind alleys turn off the main streets.

The coast of Puglia

Polignano a Mare (*left*) is similar to many other southern Puglian towns, such as Ostuni and Martina Franca, in its convoluted layout of narrow streets and dazzling white houses. The difference between them is that this is a maritime rather than a farming community. Unlike the rest of southern Italy, Puglia was drawn to the sea because the waters of the lower Adriatic teem with fish; there is still a lively local fishing industry at Polignano.

The medieval quarters of the town are built right on the cliff edge and its houses seem to emerge from the rock as if they are part of it. The lower walls of some have actually been cut from the cliff face, which falls away beneath them to the Adriatic seventy feet below. The drama is heightened by vast caverns in the cliffs, over which the houses seem to be precariously suspended.

Above Fishing along this stretch of coast still depends largely on traditions that go back several generations. Nylon has replaced plant fibre in the making of nets, and the diesel engine has taken over from sails and oars, but the technique is still the same. Trawls and seines – large nets hung vertically in the water with floats at the top and weights at the bottom – as seen in this photograph, are still put out and drawn in according to the movement of the constellations, as in the time of the Greeks. And a knowledge of the banks, shallows, currents and tides that produce the richest harvests is a lore handed down from father to son.

Salt flats, Puglia

One of the riches of Puglia in the past were the salt flats of Margherita di Savoia (*left*). Because of the value of salt they proved a tempting prey to raiders from as far away as the Venetian Republic.

New techniques of salt gathering have changed their aspect very little. The flat expanses of water broken by long straight dykes have an abstract quality from the air, particularly with a cloudless sky overhead.

Trani, Puglia

Until the fourteenth century, when its fortunes declined, Trani was an important commercial centre and trading post for merchants from Pisa, Genoa, Ravello and Amalfi. Crusaders set sail for the Holy Land from here, taking with them an image of the cathedral of San Nicola Pellegrino, one of the finest Romanesque buildings in southern Italy. It consists of an upper and a lower church, the lower one dating from the eighth century, the upper, decorated with a rose window, blind arcading and carved capitals, from 1096. Built by public subscription, which perhaps accounts for the fact that it took a hundred years to complete, the cathedral was erected in honour of a wandering pilgrim named Nicola – a charismatic figure who died in Trani and was later canonized by Pope Urban II.

The building's greatest treasure is a pair of magnificent bronze doors installed in 1179, in the reign of William II of Sicily, and set into an intricately carved stone portal reflecting the influence of the Norman kings in the south.

Le Castella, Calabria

The thirteenth-century fortress known as Le Castella, off the Ionian coast of Calabria, is remarkable for its site: settlements in southern Italy were rarely built on the shore because of the threat of raids, but here there was a port and a small town that had grown up around it, and both required protection against attack from the sea. The castle was extensively reconstructed in the sixteenth century.

La Sila, Calabria

Left The Sila massif is one of the most beautiful regions of southern Italy. The name comes from *silva*, the Latin for wood, and was applied in Roman times to the whole of the wooded uplands of the Bruttian peninsula, including the hills of Aspromonte in the 'toe'. In the Middle Ages the name came to apply only to the almost circular area between Crotone and Cosenza. Much of its forest had been destroyed by the Romans, largely to supply wood for shipbuilding, but careful control is now being exercised over cutting and replanting.

Above about 2,000 feet the olives and fruit trees of the lower slopes give way to chestnut, turkey oak and broad expanses of cereal crops. Above that again are maples and native pines, and higher still, around 4,000 feet, mostly beeches and silver fir. Snowdrops, followed by daffodils, violets and orchids, wild strawberries and delicious mushrooms grow here undisturbed, and the woods are still inhabited by hares, roe deer, martens, vipers, wild pigs and a fierce variety of wolf.

In the distant past people lived in the Sila only in summer, when sheep were brought here to graze, but villages later sprang up on the slopes and countered the power of local barons, transforming much of the pastoral land into crop-growing areas. Traces of this transformation of the highlands have survived in a few areas, one relic of the struggle between peasants and overlords being this watchtower in the fields near Robliano (*right*).

Rossano, Calabria

The city of Rossano, inland from the Gulf
of Táranto on its south-western side, was
not only a Byzantine fortress town but also
the nerve centre of the whole civil and
religious system of Byzantium in this region
of Italy. Perched high on a rock plateau
eight hundred feet up, it occupies a
spectacular site overlooking a steep gorge. It
looks almost inaccessible, and in the tenth
and eleventh centuries its vantage point
helped the Byzantines to fight off repeated
Arab attack.

The rock walls of the plateau are full of
caves which once sheltered anchorites and
hermits.

Sopramonte, Sardinia

Sopramonte, south-east of Orgosolo, is the geographical and historical heart of Sardinia. This small village of simple, circular huts, known as *pinnedda*, was a swineherds' camp, and it has survived unaltered since it was inhabited by some of Sardinia's earliest settlers.

With hardly any means of access by road or track, this desolate and mysterious region is cut off by forest and deep valleys. The mountains, the highest and bleakest on the island, are a labyrinth of caves and narrow passages, the perfect hideout of sheep-rustlers and bandits.

Tavolara Island, Sardinia

The topmost peak of the island of Tavolara offers a spectacular view of the north-east coast of Sardinia, its shoreline broken by inlets and promontories, wide bays and little islands. Facing Tavolara is the port of Olbia, the main disembarkation point for boats from Civitavecchia on the mainland.

Cape Caccia, Sardinia

One of Sardinia's most spectacular natural features, in the north-western extremity of the island, is Cape Caccia, where cliffs rise several hundred feet above the Mediterranean.

Sardinians have never felt an affinity with the sea. On the contrary, it was something to fear in the past for the easy access it offered invaders, especially during the days of Saracen raids, and this antipathy persists today. Until recently there was no need to open up this wild and empty promontory – there was nobody here. But tourists, who do not share local fears and memories, are not easily deterred, and the road to the tip of the cape was built for them. Now people come from the resort town of Alghero along the coast to enjoy the views and the cliffs, and to explore the fantastic subterranean lagoons of Neptune's Grotto, one of the most spectacular caves in the world.

Cape Testa, Sardinia (overleaf)

Sardinia's northern shoreline fragments into rocky islets and headlands around Cape Testa, which faces the yellow cliffs of Corsica. Strong winds and currents in the Strait of Bonifacio have eroded the granite, incising deep cracks in its surface. The colour of the rock ranges from deep grey to terracotta pink, and the waters are so pellucid that shapes and colours can be seen far below the surface.

Su Nuraxi, Sardinia

At Barúmini, near the regional border of Oristano and Cagliari, lies the extraordinary prehistoric village of Su Nuraxi, by far the largest settlement of a type unique to Sardinia. There are remains of about seven thousand buildings of this kind scattered over the island: known as *nuraghi*, they date from the period 1500 to 500 BC, and most of them were probably used as fortresses, watch-towers and burial places.

Su Nuraxi is exceptional both in terms of its size and in the nature of its buildings. It consists of a massive stronghold (1500-1450 BC), originally three-storeyed, with later corner towers, and a total of 396 other buildings: houses, mill chambers, baking ovens, storage houses, wells and even a bathing area have been uncovered.

The nuraghic people were mostly semi-nomadic shepherds, and to judge from the fact that each of the huts in the complex is entirely separate from its neighbour, they led independent lives within the community. However, the fact that such a large settlement existed here at all has suggested to some scholars that a change may have been in progress towards the end of the sixth century, and that the individualism of the old shepherd chiefs had by then begun to give way to a broad sense of solidarity among the island tribes, a prelude to a kind of political unity. But the arrival of the Phoenicians put an end to that forever.

Orange groves, Sardinia

On the sun-baked Campidano plain of the
south-west, agriculture is poor and harvests
scanty. Besides the aridity that afflicts much
of southern Italy, Sardinian farmers have
another enemy, the scorching wind. It is
dry, relentless and devastating, and they use
every device to outwit it. Orange groves are
hedged round with tall rustling reed barriers
to provide a sheltered oasis in which the
fruit can ripen in the hot sun and the trees
are protected from damage.

Caprera Island, Sardinia

The island of Caprera in the Maddalena
archipelago, off Sardinia's northern shore, is
a landscape of granite and blue-green sea.
Large pools of limpid water are sheltered by
outcrops of lichen-covered rock, weathered
and scarred like most of this beautiful
coastline. The sandy bays and headlands of
the Costa Smeralda lie just to the south, but
so far Caprera has escaped a tourist
invasion.

Garibaldi built a house on the island and
lived here intermittently until his death in
1882.

Arabo-Norman Palermo, Sicily
(overleaf)

The Saracens captured Palermo in AD 831,
after a year's siege and at the cost of the
lives of nearly all its 70,000 inhabitants.
Under their rule it became the capital of an
emirate and a great centre of Arab
civilization.

The other major power to make its mark
here was the Norman court of Roger II (son
of the Saracens' conqueror), who allowed
the Moslem population the freedom to
practise their religion and employed their
skills as builders and decorators. As a result
of this enlightened attitude, Palermo
achieved a brilliant synthesis of Arab and
Norman architecture.

Left The cathedral, in the heart of the city,
was founded in 1185. It has been altered
frequently, with an incongruous dome
added in the eighteenth century, but the
apse and towers at the east end, and much
of the decoration, display its Arabo-
Norman origins. One of the columns of the
Gothic porch on the south side bears an
inscription from the Koran, and derives
from the mosque which once stood on the

site of the present building. Along the far
side of the cathedral square is the
sixteenth-century Archbishop's Palace.

The Corso Vittorio Emanuele, bisecting
the centre of Palermo, exemplifies the sort
of contrasts that make up Sicily's capital: on
one side grand buildings overlook spacious
garden squares; on the other a jumble of old
houses, many of them dilapidated, are
crammed together round the dark wells of
tiny courtyards.

Right The beautiful little cloister of San
Giovanni degli Eremiti was built in the
thirteenth century, about a hundred years
after its neighbouring church had been
converted from a mosque.

The stern style brought to the island by
the Normans was softened under the
influence of the highly refined heritage left
by long years of Arab domination. In the
delicacy of these slender twin columns and
almost pointed arches can be seen this
meeting of ideas and craftsmanship from
north and south, a synthesis of cultures that
is typical of Sicily.

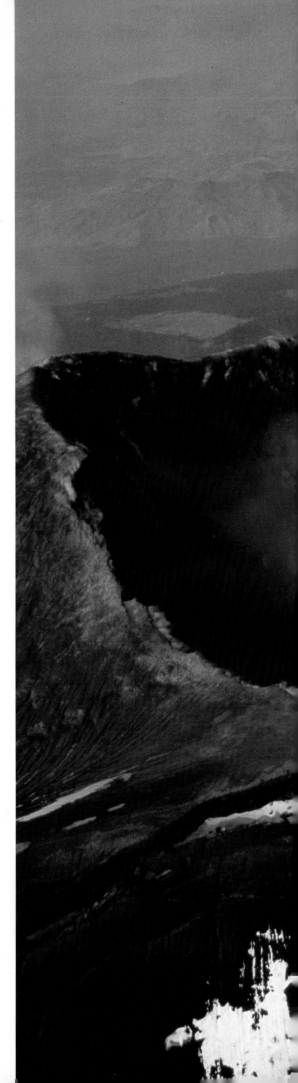

Mount Etna, Sicily

'Snow-covered Aetna, eternal dwelling of
the angry god of fire', was what Pindar
called this mountain two thousand five
hundred years ago. It is still the most active
volcano in Europe, with major eruptions
every four to twelve years, the most recent
being in 1981. It smokes constantly, and the
air round the central crater is chokingly
heavy with the fumes of sulphur. At nearly
eleven thousand feet, the summit is
snow-covered for much of the year and the
air is intensely cold. Around the active cone
are black, barren stretches of clinker and
ash, pitted with fumaroles that pour out
steam and hot gases, and scarred by craters
burned red in the heat of ancient eruptions.

It is impossible to look over the rim of
Etna's central crater and not feel awe-struck
at the power that has created this landscape
and swallowed up towns and villages as far
as the coast. But if its destructive might is
devastating, the mountain also has its
merits: the villagers on the lower slopes
have Etna to thank for the fertile soil –
wellwatered by melted snow – in which they
grow mandarins, lemons, olives, pistachios,
figs and bananas, and produce some of the
best wine on the island.

Syracuse, Sicily

The ancient city of Syracuse stands on the island of Ortygia, which is linked to the mainland by a bridge. With natural harbours to east and west, and marshland, rivers, and a long ridge to protect it from attack on its landward side, its position gave it an invaluable strategic advantage which every Mediterranean power in the ancient world endeavoured to secure. It drew the Corinthians here in 734 BC: it was they who founded the city and made it the centre of Greek dominion in Sicily for over five hundred years. Under the tyrants Dionysius I and Timoleon, Syracuse became the illustrious capital of the Greek world. But it was always at the heart of power struggles, and its history is one of endless and violent wars.

Archimedes lived here in the third century BC, and when Syracuse was under attack from the Romans he set fire to the enemy fleet by focusing the sun's rays with a system of mirrors and lenses. In spite of his ingenuity Rome succeeded in taking the city, and under Verres and Sextus Pompey, who exploited it for their personal gain, it was governed with ruthless cruelty. The Emperor Augustus restored its trade links and some of its pride, but the respite was brief: before long Syracuse was overrun by a succession of barbarians – Franks, Goths and Vandals – who were not finally thrown out until 535 AD.

When Byzantium moved its court here from Constantinople Syracuse, for a few glorious years, became the capital of the Byzantine Empire. But this brilliant interlude was followed by two hundred years of Saracen raids, culminating in the most traumatic siege the city ever endured: on 15 June 827 the Saracens arrived in Sicily from Sousse in Tunisia, led by Sinàn-Asad-el-Furàt, and launched a violent and relentless attack on the walls of Syracuse. The inhabitants of the city were reduced to cannibalism in order to survive, only to be massacred when the Arabs finally broke through.

In the words of the historian Amari, 'everything seemed still that morning, when at six o'clock all the weapons of the enemy came into play at once. They exploded like

Ragusa Ibla, Sicily

The old city of Ragusa, known as Ragusa Ibla, winds up a ridge between two river gorges, with the new town, once separate, spreading beyond it. Its steep hillside site shows off superbly the beauty and magnificence of the church of San Giorgio: built in the eighteenth century to a design of Rosario Gagliardi, it is the greatest masterpiece of Sicilian baroque. From a piazza lined with palm trees a curving stairway leads up to the flamboyant façade, where rhythm and detail and a brilliant use of convex curves and receding planes combine to create a superbly graceful effect. As it was meant to be, the church is the focus of the narrow winding streets of honey-coloured houses, but its proportions are such that it does not overpower them.

a storm bursting. The enemy rushed in and slaughtered the defenders. The fortress and the city were lost forever.' It was the end of the great Greek centre, but in 1061 the Normans arrived and drove out the Arabs for good. This was the start of a period of recovery which continued under Frederick II (in 1239 he built Castello Maniace, the fortress on the farthest tip of the island), and at last the inhabitants could breathe

more peacefully.

Two thousand seven hundred years of clashes and revolts, interspersed with periods of supreme glory, have left behind layer upon layer of civilization. The cathedral of Syracuse (its west front, just visible in the picture, stands up high on the far side of Ortygia) gives some idea of the length and complexity of the city's history: it started life as a temple to Athena, and was

one of the most magnificent temples of the ancient world. In Byzantine times it was converted into a church, but the original Doric columns still survive in the long north and south walls. The Normans made a few changes when Roger I was in power, and after a disastrous earthquake in 1693 a Baroque façade was added. The result is a reflection of changing styles and beliefs over twenty-five centuries.

Segesta, Sicily

The Greek temple at Segesta, inland from
Castellammare in the north-west of the
island, overlooks a landscape of wild hills
and deep ravines, with hardly a sign of
habitation. There was once a city here,
founded, according to Thucydides, by the
Elymians, refugees from the Trojan War.
But after incessant clashes with the Greeks,
and later domination by the Carthaginians
and Romans, it was destroyed by the
Saracens in the tenth century. The Temple
of Artemis, begun *c.* 430 BC and left
unfinished, was probably never intended as
a temple in the usual sense but as a shrine
enclosing an altar dedicated to a local cult.
The Doric columns, still unfluted, surround
a roofless open space rather than a covered
cella. The position of the temple and the
beauty of its proportions leave an indelible
impression.

Aci Trezza, Sicily

Off the shore of Aci Trezza are the lava
rocks known as Cyclops' Reefs, said to be
the boulders that the Cyclops Polyphemus
hurled after the fleeing Ulysses, who had
blinded him by thrusting a blazing stake
into his single eye.

Here, as in most of Sicily's coastal towns,
fishing is an ancient tradition – anchovies,
sardines and mackerel are in rich supply –
but there is not much fishing in Aci Trezza
nowadays: the boats in the harbour are
busy taking tourists on excursions. The
change in lifestyle is reflected in the
changing townscape; clusters of white
houses have given way to undistinguished
apartment buildings and small hotels.

Agrigento, Sicily

The temples of Agrigento are one of the finest treasures the Greeks left to Sicily.

The Doric Temple of Concord (at the top of the modern road in the background) is Italy's best-preserved Greek temple, and its majestic position makes it one of the most spectacular. It probably dates from the fifth century BC, the period of Agrigento's greatest splendour, when the city was ruled as a free state by the philosopher Empedocles. A little higher up the hill, beyond the Temple of Concord, is the ruined Temple of Juno, also built in the classical Doric style, and the few remaining columns of the Temple of Hercules – the earliest of all (late sixth century) – can be seen near the foot of the ridge. In the foreground are four re-erected columns of the so-called Temple of Castor and Pollux.

Agrigento suffered disastrously under the Carthaginians, who ransacked the town and set the temples on fire, but the Saracens and then the Normans restored some of its former glory. Today it is one of the most impressive archaeological sites in Italy.

Motya, Sicily

Between Trápani and Marsala are the three small Stagnone Islands, in a broad coastal lagoon known locally as the Big Pond. Among them is San Pantaleo, the site of the Phoenician stronghold of Motya. Perfectly sited to control the main trading route between Sicily and north Africa, it became the heart of Phoenician power in Sicily. The city expanded until it filled the island, and its necropolis had to be moved to the Sicilian coast. A road of stone blocks (which can be seen in the photograph) was laid across the floor of the lagoon, three feet below the surface, to take funeral processions and ox carts to the mainland.

The Phoenicians of Motya became so powerful that the Greeks, based in eastern Sicily, were determined to eliminate them. Repeated violent clashes culminated in a massive campaign mounted by Dionysius I from Syracuse. He savagely attacked the united Phoenician and Carthaginian army and succeeded in totally destroying the island city. In this he was helped by the submerged Phoenician road, by means of which he transported an astonishing array of weapons – catapults and flaming projectiles – that had never before been seen. Motya and its people suffered such irrevocable losses that the few survivors fled and their city was abandoned for ever.

Favignana and Fórmica, Sicily

What appear from the sky to be the ruins of a lost city are actually abandoned tufa quarries on the eastern shores of Favignana (*right*), the largest of the Égadi Islands. Stone has been quarried here since the time of the Romans, and taken to mainland Sicily to construct temples, fortresses, churches and every kind of domestic building. It is relatively simple to transport because the quarries are so near the sea.

The Égadi Islands once belonged to Marquese Pallavicino of Genoa, and he and his descendants were largely responsible for founding their economy, developing the quarries and the fishing industry, planting vineyards and building a town on Favignana. In 1875 the islands changed hands: the last of the Pallavicino family sold them to Ignazio Florio, the son of a tuna entrepreneur from Palermo. He applied his father's techniques to the tuna business in Favignana and built a processing plant there and another on the microscopic island of Fórmica (*above*). Each is a superb example of nineteenth-century industrial architecture, with arched windows and doors, more like a moorish palace than a fish cannery. Florio's son Vincenzo was a fast liver who let the business run down, and now the buildings stand empty, though the quays are still used by small fishing boats.

Between Fórmica – the name means 'ant' in Italian – and the Égadi Islands, in the background of the picture, run strong currents which bring the tuna here between April and July, the time of the famous *mattanza*, or tuna slaughter.

Index